Chinese American Children & Families

A Guide for Educators & Service Providers

Amy Lin Tan, Ph.D.

Sacramento City Unified School District

ACEI

Association for Childhood Education International
17904 Georgia Ave., Ste. 215, Olney, MD 20832
800-423-3563 • www.acei.org

Bruce Herzig, ACEI Editor
Anne Bauer, ACEI Editor
Deborah Jordan Kravitz, Design and Production

Library of Congress Cataloging-in-Publication Data

Tan, Amy Lin.
  Chinese American children and families : a guide for educators and service providers /
by Amy Lin Tan.
        p. cm.
  Includes bibliographical references.
  ISBN 0-87173-163-0 (pbk.)
  1. Chinese American children. 2. Chinese American families. I. Title.

E184.C5T358 2004
305.895'1073—dc22

                                                                      2004011203

Table of Contents

INTRODUCTION 7

CHAPTER 1
OVERVIEW OF CHINESE AMERICANS 11
  Geographic Origins **12**
  Immigration History and Reasons **13**
  Language/Linguistic Origins and Issues **15**
    Spoken Languages: Cantonese, Mandarin, and Other Dialects **15**
    Written Forms: Traditional Script, Simplified Script, and Pinyin **16**
    Characteristics of the Chinese Language **17**
  Belief Systems and Values **17**
    Confucianism **17**
    Taoism **18**
    Buddhism **18**
    Polytheism and Ancestral Worship **19**
    Animism **20**
    Christianity and Islam **20**
    Traditional Value Systems **20**
  Communication Styles **21**
    High-Context Communication Patterns **21**
    Confrontation and Refusal Avoidance **21**
    "Face" Issues and Intermediaries **21**
    Humility, Body Language, and Smiles **22**
  Naming Systems **22**
    Sequence of Family Name and Given Name **22**
    Given Name Selection **23**
    Married Name **23**
    Nicknames and Aliases **24**
    English Name **24**
  Other Relevant Information **24**
    The Chinese New Year **24**
    Cultural Considerations **26**
      Etiquette/Greetings **26**
      Eye Contact and Head Touching **26**
      Home Visiting, Gift Giving, Colors, and Numbers **26**

CHAPTER 2
FAMILY 29
  Family Composition and Structure **30**
    Extended Family and Other Cohabiting Practices **30**
    Gender Value **31**
    Kinships **31**
    Marital Roles **32**
  Marital Relationships and Parental Responsibilities **32**
  Gender-Specific Roles of Family Members **33**
  Sibling Relations **34**
  Status and Hierarchy **34**

Decision Making **35**
Communication and Interaction Styles **35**
    Parent-Child Communication and Interactions **35**
    Spousal, In-Law, and Grandparent-Grandchild Communication **36**
Relationships and Interactions With Clan and Friends **37**
Summary and Implications **37**
    Characteristics and Expectations of Chinese American Families **37**
    Familial Discord **38**
    Managing Familial Problems **39**
    Counseling Considerations and Strategies **39**

CHAPTER 3
CHILD-REARING PRACTICES 41

How Children Are Perceived **42**
    Parent-Child Relationship **42**
    Parental Roles and Responsibilities **42**
    The Child's Roles and Responsibilities **43**
    Parent-Child Communication and Interactions **44**
    Expectations of Children **44**
    Priorities for Children **45**
        Academic Achievement **45**
        Cultural Preservation **46**
        Etiquette **46**
    Education and Schooling **46**
    Perception of Birth Order and Gender **47**
    Generation and Cultural Gaps **48**
Caregiving **49**
    Caregiving and Caregivers **49**
    Grandparents and Caregiving **49**
    Baby Carriers and Baby Carrying **49**
Feeding/Food **50**
    Breast-Feeding, Bottle-Feeding, and Weaning **50**
    Baby Food **50**
    Feeders **51**
    Independent Feeding **51**
    Food and Diet **51**
    Mealtime Configuration and Family-Style Service **52**
Toilet Training/Self-Help Skills **53**
Sleeping Patterns **53**
Parenting Attitudes and Practices **54**
    The Concept of Training **54**
    Chinese-Style Parenting Practices **54**
    Parent-Child Conflicts Related to Parenting Practices **55**
    Parenting in Infancy and Early Childhood **55**
Child Discipline **56**
    Conceptualization of Discipline **56**
    Ages of Innocence and Understanding **56**
    Parameters of Acceptable and Unacceptable Behaviors **57**
    Disciplinarians **57**
    Forms of Discipline **57**
    Forms of Rewards **58**

Implications for Educators and Other Professionals   58
   Cultural Influences   58
   Intra-Group Diversity   59
   Individual and Gender Differences   60
   Relationship and Credibility Building   60

CHAPTER 4
EDUCATION 63
   Attitudes Toward Education   64
   Perception of Parental Role in the Child's Schooling   65
   Parental Perception of the Teacher's and School's Roles and Responsibilities   65
   Education System in the Homelands   66
   Similarities and Differences Between Chinese and American Schools   67
   Differences in Classroom Interactions   69
   Learning Styles of Chinese Students   71
   Linguistic Issues   72
   Academic Success and Difficulty   73
      Polarized Academic Performances   73
      Theories of Academic Success   73
      Cultural Factors Related to Academic Performance   74
         Parental Attitudes   74
         Student Attitudes   75
         Effort   75
      Academic Difficulties   76
      Chinese American Students at Risk   76
         Poverty and Distractions From Academic Focus   76
         Lack of Parental Support and Supervision   76
         Risk Factors in School and Societal Contexts   77
   Parental Pressure and Academic Stress   77
   Parental Involvement and Interactions With Teachers and the School   78
   Heritage Language School   79
   Parental Perceptions of Extracurricular Activities   81
   Implications and Recommendations   81
      Administration and Leadership   81
         Cultural Literacy and Staff Development   82
         Community Outreach and Involvement   82
         A Bilingual and Bicultural Support System   83
         Parent Leadership Empowerment   84
      Classroom Interactions   84
         Student-Teacher Relationship and Interactions   84
         Classroom Teaching-Learning Interactions   85
         Accommodating Learning Styles   85
      Counseling   86
         Indirect Service Approach   86
         Culturally Appropriate and Responsive Counseling   86
      Partnership-Building With Parents   87
         Cultural Literacy and Self-Reflection   87
         A Support System To Build Relationships   87
         Language and Culture Barriers   87
         Personal Touches and Connections   88

CHAPTER 5
HEALTH, MENTAL HEALTH, AND HEALTH CARE 89
Health Concepts and Beliefs   **90**
Views of Physical Health   **90**
Concept of Mental Health   **91**
Views on Promoting and Maintaining Health   **91**
Interpretations of Causations of Physical and Mental Illnesses   **92**
Pluralistic Assumptions of Causes of Illnesses   **92**
Multiple Suppositions of Causation of Mental Illnesses   **92**
Healers and Healing Approaches   **93**
A Pluralistic Healing System   **93**
Folk Treatments   **93**
Folk Nutrition   **94**
Food Groups and Dietary Therapy   **94**
Tonics and Vitamins   **95**
Traditional Chinese Medicine   **95**
Treatment Modalities and Diagnoses   **95**
Chinese Herbal Medications   **96**
Chinese Medicine Treatment Procedures and Techniques   **97**
Supernatural Health Care and Treatments   **97**
Issues Related to Pluralistic Healing Approaches   **98**
Mental Health Healing   **99**
Oral Hygiene and Dental Heath   **99**
Postpartum Care   **100**
Sexuality   **101**
Death and Dying   **102**
Implications for Health Care Professionals   **103**

CHAPTER 6
DISABILITIES AND INTERVENTION 105
Views of Disabilities   **106**
Causation of Disabilities   **106**
Random Events   **107**
Genetic/Hereditary Reasons   **107**
Medical Factors   **107**
Pregnancy and/or Postpartum Behaviors   **107**
Supernatural Factors   **108**
Divine Punishment   **108**
Demonic Possession   **108**
Ancestral or Fengshui Factors   **108**
Perceptions and Attitudes Toward Intervention   **108**
Help-Seeking and Intervention   **109**
Collaboration With Professionals   **109**
Implications and Recommendations   **110**
Concept of Developmental Services and Special Education   **110**
Cultural and Linguistic Interpreters   **111**
Relationship-Building, Trust, and Face-Saving   **111**
Communication and Interaction Styles   **112**
Parental Gratitude and Reciprocity   **112**
Formality, Courtesy, and Other Cultural Considerations   **112**

REFERENCES 114

Introduction

As an educator who was educated in Taiwan and the United States, and who has worked in both education systems, I am well-versed in their educational practices. More important, I am also fully aware of the needs of educators and other service providers in America when it comes to working with minority children and families. In my nearly 20 years of experience coordinating services for children and families in California, I have long realized the limited availability of multicultural information and resources. The information is even more scarce or non-existent as it pertains to working with Asian Americans. With the increasing number of Chinese Americans in the United States, it is more and more apparent that a book with insightful and pertinent information intended for educators and other practitioners is needed. As I give presentations at conferences on working with children and families of diverse backgrounds, I am often asked by audience members to share what I presented in writing. Being an immigrant who is deeply connected to the immigrant community yet practices in the mainstream culture, I feel a moral as well as a professional obligation to bridge the gap by putting down in book format what I know, and what educators and service providers need to know, regarding working with Chinese American children and families. Combining bicultural insight and professional experiences while weaving in available literature, this book brings forth a perspective that straddles two worlds to give educators and other professionals the tools needed for providing culturally sensitive services.

While the information presented in this book is pertinent to Chinese Americans, with relevant applications to East Asian Americans and

Southeast Asian Americans, the book does have a broader application to all cultures. The content of this book certainly is Chinese-specific; the topics, however, are universal. As the world becomes smaller and smaller, cultural proficiency and competency become more and more a necessity for educators and other professionals serving children and families of diverse backgrounds. Information and resources may not always keep pace with demographic changes and the resulting needs of educators and professionals. Given the aspect of universality in service provision regardless of culture, educators and service providers frustrated with sparse or non-existent information and resources regarding working with children and families of a specific culture may want to go beyond the cultural specifics and take a different and broader perspective. The structure of each chapter in this book, as well as the topics and subtopics covered therein, shed some light on the aspect of universality. Utilizing the carefully and thoughtfully organized headings and subheadings, the readers will have clues to help them start researching cultural specific information and also have the tools to map out strategies for tackling the issues at hand, regardless of culture.

Undertaking a writing project covering a wide range of interrelated topics has both advantages and risks, especially when a wide range of ages is encompassed. I have tried to present the pertinent information that educators and service providers need to know as comprehensively and yet as succinctly as possible. Every effort was made to strike a balance and meet the perceived needs of the audience. Nonetheless, what I presented may be too lengthy for readers who only need very basic information, while others might appreciate more detailed or more in-depth information. In the implications and recommendations sections, I offer primarily general suggestions. The main focus of this book is to present educators and service professionals with critical relevant, pertinent, and comprehensive information.

Trusting that educators and other professionals can easily come up with their own conclusions based on the information shared, I believe in leaving the professional decisions to the professionals. In sum, I am aware of the dilemma of comprehensiveness versus brevity and the shortcomings associated with that dilemma. I can only hope that the readers will use their own ingenuity and professional discretion to process and internalize the information presented. For those readers who desire more information, the extensive references at the end of the book offer leads for further reading. I also hope my colleagues in education and experts in other service delivery areas will come forth with more publications or more in-depth, single-discipline publications concerning working with Chinese American children and families. The scarcity of the information highlights the need for the publications.

Although I have tried to present the information related to Chinese Americans as accurately as possible, I am aware of the inherent danger of over-generalization and over-simplification. There is tremendous intra-group diversity among so-called Chinese Americans. Many variables contribute to the diversity. Generally speaking, personality, immigration reason, birthplace or region of origin, home dialect, education level, English proficiency, acculturation extent, adherence to Chinese traditions, economic situation, social status, and place of residence in the United States are factors to consider when working with Chinese Americans. As the cliché goes, there is no typical Chinese American, nor a typical Chinese American family. Culture itself is dynamic rather than static.

Chinese in America, for the most part, are interacting in a bicultural social context. To some extent, Chinese Americans are more or less at a transitional stage in the acculturation process, undergoing constant changes and adaptations. In light of this, readers are reminded to exercise their professional discretion when interpreting and applying the information presented in the book. When working with children and their families, it is important, not to mention wise, to always consider them as individuals first. When applying the information in this book, readers must take the diversity variables into account. Also keep in mind that the information presented is more representative of less acculturated Chinese Americans. These points reiterated, it is the sincere hope that the author has done a genuine service to both Chinese Americans and the professionals who work with them.

Chapter 1
Overview of Chinese Americans

Geographic Origins   12
Immigration History and Reasons   13
Language/Linguistic Origins and Issues   15
    Spoken Languages: Cantonese, Mandarin, and Other Dialects   15
    Written Forms: Traditional Script, Simplified Script, and Pinyin   16
    Characteristics of the Chinese Language   17
Belief Systems and Values   17
    Confucianism   17
    Taoism   18
    Buddhism   18
    Polytheism and Ancestral Worship   19
    Animism   20
    Christianity and Islam   20
    Traditional Value Systems   20
Communication Styles   21
    High-Context Communication Patterns   21
    Confrontation and Refusal Avoidance   21
    "Face" Issues and Intermediaries   21
    Humility, Body Language, and Smiles   22
Naming Systems   22
    Sequence of Family Name and Given Name   22
    Given Name Selection   23
    Married Name   23
    Nicknames and Aliases   24
    English Name   24
Other Relevant Information   24
    The Chinese New Year   24
    Cultural Considerations   26
        Etiquette/Greetings   26
        Eye Contact and Head Touching   26
        Home Visiting, Gift Giving, Colors, and Numbers   26

The largest Asian American group with the longest presence in the United States, Chinese Americans also have had the highest visibility. Prominent Chinese Americans in various fields have captured the attention of the public and have been promoted as role models by both the Chinese community and the American mainstream. Among these influential people are Elaine Chao (U.S. Secretary of Labor), Gary Locke (Governor of Washington), David Wu (Oregon Congressman), Chang-Lin Tien (late Chancellor of the University of California, Berkeley), Connie Chung (TV journalist), Michelle Kwan (figure skating champion), Yo Yo Ma (cellist), and several Nobel Laureates and astronauts.

Although most Americans love Chinese food, watch Kung Fu movies, and use merchandise manufactured in China, not too many can truthfully say they are knowledgeable about China or the Chinese culture. With 2.88 million, or 1 percent, of the total U.S. population being of Chinese heritage, mainstream Americans and other minorities should learn about their Chinese American neighbors. Service providers, be they educators, health care and mental health professionals, law enforcement personnel, or social workers, especially need to become knowledgeable about the Chinese American people with whom they work.

This book is intended to help educators and service providers work with Chinese American children and families by offering detailed descriptions of common Chinese beliefs and practices concerning child rearing, education, health, mental health, and disabilities. This section will provide some pertinent basic background information regarding geographic origins, immigration history, linguistic issues, belief systems, communication styles, and naming systems. This information is necessarily generalized and cannot be interpreted as true for all Chinese or all Chinese Americans. It should serve only as an aid in enhancing understanding of the cultural characteristics that may contribute to a Chinese child's or family's mindset and behavior.

Geographic Origins

Most first-generation Chinese Americans came from China, Hong Kong, and Taiwan. Some originated in Vietnam, and a smaller number emigrated from other Southeast Asian countries, including Cambodia, Laos, Malaysia, Myanmar (Burma), the Philippines, Singapore, and Thailand. Additionally, a very small number of Chinese entered the United States via Central and South America and other places around the world.

Hong Kong and Taiwan are historically part of China, and are populated primarily by Han Chinese. Before the 1980s, most of the Chinese American immigrants from China came from the Guangdong (Kwangtung) Province of southeast China, near Hong Kong. Since the 1980s, Chinese from Mainland China have come to the United States from various major cities in China. The ethnic Chinese from Southeast Asian countries are descendants of Chinese immigrants who emigrated there from southeast China, mostly from the coastal Guangdong and Fujian provinces. Their ancestors may have been in Southeast Asia since the 1800s or for only a few decades. Many Vietnamese and Cambodian refugees who came to the United States after the Indochina Wars are ethnic Chinese. The forefathers of those from Central and South America and other parts of the world mostly emigrated from Guangdong decades ago.

Immigration History and Reasons

Generally speaking, Chinese people are not adventurous in comparison to other ethnic groups. In fact, Chinese people have a strong tradition of feeling a bond to the land where they are born and raised and supposed to be buried. Nevertheless, the Chinese have had a presence in the United States for more than two centuries. Chinese first arrived in the United States as early as 1785 (Chinn, 1967; Lee, 1998). Greater numbers of Chinese immigrants came to the United States in different waves.

The first wave of Chinese immigrants came as sojourners for economic reasons, with the intention to return home, between the second half of the 1800s and early 1900s. These impoverished bachelors, who mostly originated from the rural areas of the Guangdong Province, came to work as railroad laborers, miners, and farmhands. Many of them did not amass a fortune as hoped, and they eventually settled on the West Coast and along the railroad towns. Between 1920 and 1942, with the immigration law change, many first-wave laborers were able to send for their wives and children. During this period, the second wave of small business families occurred.

After World War II, another wave of Chinese, mainly from Taiwan and Hong Kong, came to the United States pursuing higher education or family reunification. Those who came as students often stayed after graduation and sponsored more family members to enter the United States. Better economic opportunities, freedom, and democracy, as well as political stability, were the incentives for these immigrants to seek employment and remain in the States.

The 1965 Immigration and Nationality Act and its 1990 extension also resulted in a dramatic increase of Chinese immigration, mostly from Hong Kong and Taiwan. The policy abolished race-based entry quotas and gave priority to family reunification and educated, skilled professionals. During the late 1970s and early 1980s, the ethnic Chinese merchant class in Vietnam and Cambodia were forced to leave those countries as communist rule prevailed. Many of these "boat people" who had survived ordeals on the open sea entered the United States as refugees.

Since the 1970s and throughout the 1990s, some well-to-do families in Taiwan and Hong Kong also emigrated to pursue business ventures, for the sake of their children's education, or for political reasons. Often, investments in business ventures were easier ways to obtain immigrant status for the whole family. Excellent and plentiful higher education opportunities, less stressful competition for college entrance, and the fear of Hong Kong's return to China or of Taiwan's political instability were common underlying reasons for immigrating to the United States.

With the normalization of diplomatic relations between the U.S. and China in 1979 and China's reform and opening up in the 1980s, the number of immigrants from major cities of Mainland China also has increased

at a steady rate. U.S. Immigration and Naturalization Service data indicates that in 1999 and 2000, immigrants from the People's Republic of China constituted the second largest group of legal immigrants, next to Mexicans (Yu, 2002). In 2002, 61,000 Chinese immigrants arrived from Mainland China (Kong, 2003). Most of them came to pursue higher education or join their families. In addition, large numbers of students continued to come from China, Hong Kong, and Taiwan annually. As did students in the previous generations, many of these Chinese students chose to remain in the States upon graduation. Other overseas Chinese, especially those from Central and South America and Southeast Asia, also came to do business, to study, or to unite with families (Chan, 1998; Chang, 2003; Lee, 1998; Matocha, 1998; Takaki, 1989; Wong & Lopez, 1995).

All of these immigrants of Chinese descent and their descendants make up the 2.88 million Chinese Americans, the largest Asian American ethnic group. Twenty percent of Asian Americans are of Chinese descent, constituting roughly 1 percent of the U.S. population (Xiao, 2002). The number reflects a huge jump in 10 years from 1.6 million people, or 0.7 percent of the total population, according to the 1990 Census. The states with the highest concentration of Chinese Americans are: Hawaii (14.1 percent, or 170,803); California (3.3 percent, or 1,122,187); New York (2.4 percent, or 451,859); Massachusetts (1.5 percent or 92,380); and New Jersey and Washington (each with 1.3 percent, or 110,263 and 75,884, respectively). The cities with the largest concentration of Chinese Americans are Monterey Park (45 percent), San Marino (44 percent), Arcadia (37 percent), San Gabriel (37 percent), and Alhambra (36 percent), all in southern California. Quincy, Massachu-

setts, is the city on the East Coast with the highest percentage (11 percent) of Chinese American residents. The cities with the largest numbers of residents of Chinese ancestry are San Francisco (160,947); the boroughs of Queens (147,037), Brooklyn (125,358), and Manhattan (91,588) in New York City; and Los Angeles (73,868).

Language / Linguistic Origins and Issues

China is a huge country, with a population that includes 56 nationalities. The Han is the overall majority, constituting nearly 92 percent of the total population ("Cultures of minority groups," 2003; Matocha, 1998). Each Chinese ethnic nationality has its own spoken language and dialect; there are 21 written languages and 62 vernaculars in use in China ("Cultures of minority groups," 2003). When people refer to the "Chinese language," however, usually they mean the language used by the Han Chinese. According to the 2000 U.S. Census (Lee, 2002), Chinese trails only Spanish in terms of a foreign language commonly spoken in the United States. Eighty-one percent of Chinese American families reported in the census that they used Chinese at home.

Spoken Languages: Cantonese, Mandarin, and Other Dialects

The Han language encompasses many dialects; the differences are often significant and more than merely accents, and thus they are often mutually unintelligible. The single written Chinese language provides unity. Most Chinese Americans speak either the Cantonese or Mandarin dialect. Cantonese used to be the predominant language of Chinatowns across America. A gradual shift from Cantonese to Mandarin, however, has been taking place, corresponding to the change of place origin of Chinese immigrants in the last 15 years (Kong, 2003). Cantonese is the dialect spoken in Guangzhou (Canton), the provincial capital of Guangdong. Families originating from Hong Kong, Gurangdong, and Vietnam, as well as some Chinese from Malaysia, Singapore, the Philippines, and Central and South America, are Cantonese speakers. Some of them also may speak Mandarin. Those from rural areas near Guangzhou speak a sub-dialect of Cantonese called Toi San.

The earliest Chinese immigrants were predominantly speakers of Toi San (Taishan, Taishanese), and Toi San continues to have a presence in Chinese American communities, including San Francisco and Sacramento. Immigrants from other parts of China and Taiwan usually can speak Mandarin fluently, although they may use a noticeably different dialect at home. Families originally from Wenzou and Fuzhou who live in New York City and its vicinity speak their own distinct dialects. Families originating from Taiwan also may speak Taiwanese, a Min dialect, also known as Fujianese or Hokkienese. Fujianese and its related dialect, Chaozhou (Chiuchao), may be the home dialect of Chinese from Southeast Asia, especially Cambodia, Malaysia, Myanmar, the Philippines, Singapore, and Thailand.

Mandarin is the Beijing-based dialect spoken in the north, west, and southwest regions by 70 percent of the population in China. It is the most widely used dialect (Li & Thompson, 1981); minor regional differences in accents occur, but usually they are mutually intelligible. Called *Putonghua* or *Guoyu*, meaning "common language" or "national language" in China and Taiwan, respectively, Mandarin is the official medium of communication and instruction in China and Taiwan. Overseas Chinese schools in Southeast Asia, Korea, and Japan, and Chinese heritage language schools/classes in the United States also use Mandarin for instruction. Some Chinese schools in the United States that are established for children from Cantonese-speaking families, however, use Cantonese instead. The desire to maintain close relationships with Cantonese-speaking relatives, parents' limited proficiency in Mandarin, and concerns about lack of reinforcement and usage at home are the main reasons for continuing the use of Cantonese as the medium of instruction in these schools.

Written Forms: Traditional Script, Simplified Script, and Pinyin

While there is only one written Chinese language, there are differences in script. In a recent extensive effort to eradicate illiteracy, China promoted a simplified form of Chinese characters. Taiwan, Hong Kong, and most other Chinese communities elsewhere, such as in the United States, continue to use the traditional style of Chinese. The simplified Chinese, as the name suggests, is basically a simplified form of Chinese script with a reduced number of strokes. For a traditional style reader and writer, it is merely a matter of getting used to the simplified system. People who have learned only the simplified style, however, find it more difficult to make the transition to the traditional form.

In addition to the simplified writing system, a phonetic form of writing, *Pinyin*, was developed in China to teach the pronunciation of *Putonghua* and transliterate Chinese ideograms into English. Using the Roman alphabet, *Pinyin* is similar to the International Phonetic Alphabet (IPA). For example, the national capital is spelled as Beijing in *Pinyin* nowadays. However, older systems of transliteration are still in use outside China and thus account for the confusion of different spellings for the same word, such as Beijing and Peking (meaning, literally, "northern capital" in Chinese). Since its creation in the 1950s, *Pinyin* has been emphasized in China and taught in primary grades to encourage a standardization of *Putonghua* as the official language.

Characteristics of the Chinese Language

Classified as a Sino-Tibetan language by linguists, the Chinese language is monosyllabic, tonal, and non-inflectional. The traditional form of the Chinese writing system is graphic, not alphabetic. It was developed more than 3,000 years ago but has changed very little. Chinese characters are either pictography, ideography, or phonography. The symbols represent concepts, rather than phonemes. In this way, speakers of different vernaculars can read the same written languages. The writing script served not only as the means of communication for different Chinese dialect speakers, but also as the writing system for Japanese and Korean. Accustomed to the lack of inflection and derivation, and the logographic writing systems, of the Chinese language, Chinese speakers find it challenging to learn English (Buckley, 1997; Chi, 1999).

Belief Systems and Values

The religious-philosophical systems of Confucianism, Taoism, and Buddhism form the foundation of Chinese beliefs and values. Although each system is distinctive with its own doctrine and philosophy, these three belief systems have blended into one unique belief and value system that dominates the spiritual practices and ideological influences of the Chinese people. Throughout the past 2,500 years, elements of each system and the mixture of all three have guided, regulated, and comforted Chinese and other Asian people and undergirded all aspects of Chinese and Asian lives from birth to death.

Although the traditional belief and value systems were suppressed under the superimposition of communism, their influences have been resurfacing since the 1980s. Thanks to political, economic, and social reforms, religion has been revived and traditional belief and value systems have been re-emphasized in China. The discussion below regarding belief systems and values suggests a broad application. Bear in mind that some leveling is inevitable. Sensitivity to each and every Chinese American must supplement the information discussed.

Confucianism

Confucianism has been the most influential force prescribing the codes of conduct to maintain social order in the Chinese society. Human relationships are the theme of Confucius's teaching and his prescription for a stable society. Confucius's goal was not religious salvation, but rather the cultivation of virtuous, perfect gentlemen who seek to attain the five virtues of benevolence, righteousness, ritual and etiquette, wisdom, and trustworthiness. Confucius discussed the rectification of the five cardinal relationships (ruler-minister, parent-child, husband-wife, siblings, and friends), describing how each is to behave within their roles. He stressed the importance of integrity, loyalty, and reciprocity. Central to all the virtues is filial piety: the duties of respecting and obeying one's parents, taking care of one's aged parents, striving to bring honor to the family name, and performing the ceremonial duties of ancestral worship (Major, 1989).

Taoism

Taoism, based on the philosophy of Laozi (Lao Tsu), emphasizes the need to transcend artificial human culture and maintain harmony with nature. Taoism stresses natural spontaneity, simplicity, passiveness, and avoidance of contrived activity. It encourages cultivation of inner strength and practicing of meditation. Taoism also elaborates on the counterbalancing forces of yin (passive, female, spirit) and yang (active, masculine, worldly) and the five elements in the universe: gold, wood, water, fire, and earth. Natural phenomena are interpreted in terms of the interactions between the yin and yang forces and the dynamics of the five elements. Originally a passive naturalistic philosophy, Taoism has evolved into a widely practiced religion, incorporating elements of Buddhism and assimilating the early Chinese belief in alchemy. Its elaborate rituals and supernatural practices sometimes are considered superstitious, magical, and animistic. In fact, many animistic rituals derive their origins from Taoist practices (Major, 1989; Porter, 1983).

Buddhism

Founded in India by Sakyamuni, Buddhism has been the most popular and widely practiced religion among all imported religions in Chinese society. The Buddhism practiced in China is the Mahayana (or the Great Vehicle Buddhism), which professes universal salvation and maintains a well-structured cleric system. The Buddhism practiced in China also is known as Zen Buddhism, which is strongly influenced by Taoism.

According to Buddhism,

life is governed by karma, the belief that a person's fate is determined by his or her actions in previous lives. The endless life cycles of birth, aging, sickness, and death are interpreted as cycles of suffering. The Buddhist's goal is to reach immortal enlightenment in order to end the cycle of reincarnation and suffering. Hence, Buddhism teaches its followers the basic principles of the Four Noble Truths: all life entails suffering, suffering is caused by human desire, suffering can be eliminated by extinguishing desire, and following the Eightfold Path can eliminate desire. The Eightfold Path consists of right view, right thinking, right speech, right action, right living, right effort, right attention, and right meditation (Bosrock, 1994; Major, 1989). Thus, Buddha's teachings shed light on the roots of human suffering and offer solutions to realize the awakening.

Rooted in self-respect and respect for others, Buddhist moral precepts teach its followers to be humanistic, fatalistic, nonviolent, pessimistic, and anti-materialistic (Yeung & Lee, 1997). According to one recent report, there are approximately 300 Chinese Buddhist temples in the United States (Zhao, 2002).

Polytheism and Ancestral Worship

Together, the three belief systems of Confucianism, Taoism, and Buddhism are called the "three teachings." Embraced and reinforced by a polytheistically and collectively oriented Chinese society, the three systems complement each other and are practiced simultaneously, along with ancestral worship and animism. A Chinese person may identify himself or herself as a Buddhist, but also may go to a Taoist temple and perform ancestral worship on a daily basis. In many households, a family shrine occupies a prominent spot in the living room, where the ancestral tablet is placed alongside a statue of a Buddha, a Taoist image, and statues or images of other deities. It is also quite common to find various gods and deities in the same temple.

The practice of ancestral worship, derived from Confucianism, is a form of remembrance and paying respect. It serves as a communication channel and social link between departed ancestors and living descendants, or between the world of men and the world of spirits (Chan, 1998; Chen, 1988). Ancestral worship is both an obligation and a privilege. The belief in mutual interdependence and the interactions between those living in the yin and yang worlds strengthen family relationships and intergenerational ties. Although some families do not maintain this tradition, a family ancestral shrine on the wall or an altar in the living room is a common sight in Chinese homes, especially in Taiwan, rural China, and Southeast Asia. A family shrine usually holds portraits of the family's most recent ancestors and written acknowledgments of more remote ancestors. An incense holder and one to three small wine cups are placed in front of the portraits.

Some Chinese may not keep an ancestral shrine in their homes or perform ancestral worship all year-round, but will pay respect to their ancestors on ancestral death days and important Chinese holidays. A temporary shrine or altar is set up a few times a year just for such occasions. Performing the duty of ancestral worship, especially on the Chinese New Year, is a tradition that even many Christian Chinese follow. The ceremony itself has been simplified in recent decades. It usually involves setting up a table laden with food offerings and incense in front of the ancestral tablet or shrine, and assembling family members to bow or kowtow to the ancestral photos and/or tablets under the leadership of the head of the household. Prayers are murmured to communicate to the ancestors. Gravesite worshiping is also carried out, especially on "The Grave-sweeping Day," commonly known as the Qingming Festival, which is on April 5 in the Gregorian calendar.

In the United States, ancestral worship is not practiced as much as in China, Hong Kong, and Taiwan. Some newly arrived, more traditional families with rural backgrounds do keep a family shrine and continue the tradition. Some Chinese American families take care of the souls of their departed forebears by keeping a soul plate in one of the 300 Buddhist temples in the United States (Zhao, 2002). This arrangement places the ancestral souls in the company of the deities residing in the temple, and is convenient for the living who wish to pay their respects and make offerings. The clan halls or family associations in the Chinatowns of major cities hold an annual ancestral worship ceremony shortly after the Chinese New Year, or on special occasions, such as when a dignitary visits from afar. In recent years, virtual ancestral worshiping has sprung up on the Internet, and the practice has been encouraged, both in the homelands and overseas.

Animism

Animism also is commonly practiced, especially in the rural areas of Asia and among less-educated people. Animism may not be practiced on a regular basis, but it is not unusual to see a makeshift shrine with offerings under a tree in the countryside in China, Taiwan, and Southeast Asian Chinese communities. Believing in the magic power possessed by the spirits living in a tree or any object, an animist will set up a simple altar with offerings to appease the spirits or ask for their blessing or protection. The influence of animism on Chinese Americans may be found in interpretations placed on the causality of illness, disabilities, or other misfortunes, but animism is not commonly practiced in the United States.

Christianity and Islam

While there are no data available concerning the percentage of Christian and Islam followers among the Chinese population, it is safe to say that the number is relatively small, although both religions have had a long presence in China. Islam was introduced by Arab traders in the seventh century and Christianity in the 16th century by European missionaries. In China, there are many more Muslims than Christians, as the non-Han ethnic minorities in the northwest regions bordering Central Asia are all Muslims.

By contrast, hardly any Chinese Americans are Muslim, while the percentage of Chinese Americans following the Christian faith is much higher than that of the Chinese in China or Taiwan. More than 1,000 Chinese Christian churches of various denominations can be found in the United States, offering services in different Chinese dialects and in English (Ly, 2003). Churches offer the Chinese community not only religious sanctuary but also socialization opportunities. Most Chinese churches also offer Chinese language school for school-age children.

Traditional Value Systems

The Confucian virtues and codes of conduct, the Taoist doctrines, and the Buddhist Eightfold Path and moral precepts discussed in the preceding section provide a clearly delineated value system by which Chinese people abide. Additionally, there are Chinese traditional cultural values pertaining to family, education, human relations, and other virtues. Values regarding family and education will be discussed in the family and education sections. Values about human relations and other virtues are reviewed below.

The Confucian and Taoist teachings place a high value on pursuing and maintaining harmonious relationships with people and nature. Preservation of harmony is achieved by being mindful of one's own position in a group, respecting others, conforming to the rules of propriety, restraining emotion, avoiding confrontation, and by being accommodating and tolerant. Consistent with a collectivist orientation, character traits of modesty, humility, self-sacrifice, conformity, patience, endurance, and perseverance, along with Confucianism-based virtues of industriousness, thrift, deferred gratification, respect for elders, family obligations, and reverence for learning and teachers, are greatly valued (Chan, 1998; Cheng, 1999; Huntsinger, Schoeneman & Ching, 1994; Siu, 1992a; Zhang & Carrasquillo, 1995).

Behavioral thematic analyses of moral values reflected in Chinese textbooks confirmed similar value orientations (Ridley, Godwin, & Doolin, 1971, cited in Chen, 1989).

Communication Styles

High-Context Communication Patterns

Influenced by religious teachings, traditional value systems, and a collectivist orientation, Chinese communication styles rely heavily on contextual cues (Chan, 1998; Hall, 1977; Huang, 1993). In contrast with the mainstream, low-context communication patterns, Chinese ways of communication often appear to be very confusing or even deceptive. Communication, to Chinese people, is more than merely exchanging information or making a statement. Rather, it also serves as a way of engaging someone, a means of forging an interpersonal relationship. Circumstance, timing, subtle environmental cues (such as surroundings and seating arrangements), and nonverbal elements (such as tone of voice, facial expression, gestures, and eye movement) all carry significant weight in discourse. Chinese use complex rules of codified language and differential speech to communicate with different people of different statuses in different situations.

Communication is receiver-oriented and discretion is emphasized. Often, the discourse itself is very implicit and indirect. Cues embedded in the codified language and differential speech are important signals conveying subtle but critical messages. For example, when the polite and respectful form of *"nin"* (you) instead of the regular *"ni"* (you) is used in the discourse, the sender is conveying a message of respect and politeness toward the receiver.

Confrontation and Refusal Avoidance

Because maintaining harmony is critical in interpersonal relationships and disagreements are interpreted as personal confrontations rather than intellectual confrontations, Chinese people put forth considerable effort to avoid directly offending others. In conversations, Chinese people may consciously or unconsciously display verbal hesitancy and ambiguity as well as avoidance of critical remarks. An affirmative "Yes" or a string of "Yes. Yes. Yes." is a polite way of maintaining the engagement of the discourse. It may only imply that "I hear you" or "I am listening, keep going" instead of "I agree with you." It is hard for Chinese people to reply with a flat "No," especially to authority figures. Therefore, indirect refusals are often voiced in disguise. "I will see," "I will try," and "maybe" are examples of polite, diplomatic, and tactful ways of avoiding a negative response. In the meantime, some people may exhibit behaviors of silence, lack of eye contact, and passivity in the discourse. These seemingly non-engaging behaviors are actually signs of respect, especially toward elders or authority figures (Chan, 1998; Huang, 1993; Sue & Sue, 1991).

"Face" Issues and Intermediaries

The Chinese culture dictates using discretion and refraining from expressing strong emotions while engaging in communication. Chinese consider themselves "thin-skinned." To avoid "losing face" (feeling that one's positive social value has been damaged) or feeling uncomfortable or embarrassed, an intermediary often is asked to serve as a go-between to convey one's message instead of having a direct, open, honest, and straightforward discourse with the person or party involved. Confrontation must be avoided at all cost. Rather than taking a direct approach on an issue involving a grudge, both sides often harbor the bad feelings and ask an intermediary to convey those feelings to the other side. An intermediary also is solicited as a liaison to facilitate communication when an issue of "face" is involved. When a confrontation cannot be avoided, the parties involved solicit an intermediary to smooth things over.

Humility, Body Language, and Smiles

Humility and modesty are highly regarded virtues; hence, boasting is considered to be in bad taste, and assertiveness is inappropriate. It is customary for Chinese to self-deprecate or downplay self-worth while at the same time giving others undeserved, upgraded recognition. People often go out of their way to be humble, having been brought up to always consider others first. Chinese are mindful of avoiding assertiveness in pursuit of one's own interests, but are careful to consider others' interests. When interacting with authority figures, Chinese people tend to be very polite and use formal or ritualized language. Quite a bit of polite but "not to the point" talking may occur before getting to the main point. Respect toward authority may be intentionally or unconsciously expressed by one's body language, such as smiling, repeated head-nodding, avoiding eye contact, sitting at the edge of the chair, taking the least desirable seat, and maintaining a stiff and erect posture.

Chinese are not overtly emotionally expressive; nevertheless, the nonverbal behavior of smiling is utilized frequently to communicate different messages under different circumstances. A smile is appropriate for greeting and welcoming guests and for situations in which a verbal expression is neither needed nor appropriate. A smile is also a bashful response to a compliment, as some Chinese are not accustomed to being complimented and feel uneasy replying with a "thank you." A smile also may be a prelude to asking for a favor or camouflage to cover up embarrassment. A smile might be a nonverbal substitute for saying "I am sorry" for a minor matter, such as being late. While most of the messages that a smile conveys are relatively easy for non-Chinese to comprehend, the substitute of a smile for an apology often causes misunderstanding.

The aforementioned communication styles are, of course, generalizations. It is crucial to consider acculturation, education levels, English proficiency, and other factors concerning individual differences when considering this information.

Naming Systems

Sequence of Family Name and Given Name

The Chinese naming system is quite different from what many Westerners are accustomed to in terms of the sequence of the given and family name and methods of giving names. In a collectivist society with a strong emphasis on the family unit rather than on the individual, the family name precedes the given name. Consider, for example, *Wang Dahua's* (or *Wang Da-Hua's, Wang Da Hua's*) name. Wang is the surname (family) name, the so-called "last name" in the Western sense. *Dahua* is the given name, most likely selected and given by his parents. The family name preceding the given name signifies that *Wang Dahua* is first and foremost a Wang.

In the United States, Chinese Americans follow local custom and reverse the order of the surname, given name sequence to follow the Western first name, last name sequence. Thus, *Wang Dahua* becomes *Dahua Wang.* There are legal reasons to follow the English sequence; nobody wants to tangle with government agencies when it comes to identity issues. It is much easier just to follow the mainstream.

Because Chinese American families use their home dialects to transliterate their

Chinese names into English, and because of the varying Romanized transliteration systems or orthographies available, the same Chinese surnames may be transliterated differently. For example, the different spellings of the Chinese family name of *Chan, Chen, Chin, Chinn, Tan,* and *Tran* share the same Chinese character and, in fact, belong to the same clan. On the other hand, the same Roman spelling of a family name does not necessarily indicate the same Chinese character of the same family name. For example, two Chinese surnames share the same transliteration spelling *Tan*.

Given Name Selection

Most Chinese people's given names consist of two characters (*Dahua, Da-hua,* or *Da Hua*). In Mainland China, a standardized way of utilizing Pinyin for transliterating names puts the two-part given name together into one word, as in *Dahua*. In other Chinese communities, given names often are hyphenated or transliterated into two parts, such as *Da-hua* or *Da Hua*. They go together as a unit and should not be separated into two parts and perceived as a "first name" and a "middle name." Immigrant Chinese with a given name that is transliterated into a two-part name (like *Da Hua*) often feel that their identity is being chopped up and reduced in half when called by one word only. They most likely would not protest or correct people, but would merely go along quietly, although it does not quite make sense to them to be given only a half identity. One of these two names, usually the first one, may be a generation name that was prescribed in the family book generations ago. In such cases, all paternal cousins of the same generation share the same generation name. Only one word is selected by parents to add on to the generation name to complete the given name. Some Chinese,

however, have only one word in their given name. Giving children a "single name" (i.e., only one character for a given name) is a trend that gains popularity from time to time.

Given names are carefully selected with parents' aspirations and expectations for the child in mind. A respected elder or an astrologer may be consulted to give advice on naming a child. The meaning of the name is the primary consideration when selecting a name. Moral virtues, personality traits, wisdom, health, good looks, wealth and rank, and feminine qualities are common considerations guiding parents in naming a child. Occasionally, a child may be named after historical events, according to the time of birth or the Taoist five elements of the universe (Lin, 1988; Liu, 1996). Thus, a name that may sound odd or seemingly unpronounceable to a non-Chinese person carries great meaning and significance. A Chinese person would welcome attempts to learn how the name was given and what the significance is.

Naming a child after a relative of the senior generation, as is common in Western cultures, is rare. Gender differences in names usually are distinct as aspirations and expectations for sons and daughters tend to be gender-specific. However, there are some gender-neutral names, as well as lofty and abstract names absent of "earthly" aspirations or expectations. Like single names, abstract names gain popularity from time to time.

Married Name

A Chinese woman keeps her maiden name after marriage. Traditionally, the mother's clan (surname) name is noted in the biography of a famous person to acknowledge the maternal lineage. In America, Chinese women often opt to follow the mainstream practice by dropping their maiden names and taking up their husbands' surnames in order to avoid confusion and misunderstanding.

Nicknames and Aliases

Sometimes, a baby name or a pet name may be given to a child, which may become a nickname that sticks with the child. Other times, a nickname may be given to an older child by people other than family members. In the past, it was a common practice to give a boy a "school name" upon school entrance, and that school name was used by schoolmates and teachers. It also was common among the literate to select one's own poetic name for use with friends. Thus, several aliases could be used in a lifetime. This practice is no longer used, but selecting an English name and being known by an English name is more common now.

English Name

Many Chinese Americans adopt an English name, for several reasons: being born in America, wanting to be like Americans, just wanting to have an English name, wanting to belong, disliking one's original Chinese name, and wishing to avoid a conspicuously ethnic name. Some people find that their Chinese name is too difficult for Americans to pronounce. Instead of answering to a strange-sounding, mispronounced name that is not really theirs, they choose to pick an English name of their own liking, much like picking a stage name or a pen name. They may enjoy this opportunity, as they did not have a say in their original name.

Another reason to choose an English name is a matter of convenience and practicality. When following the egalitarian and casual mainstream practice of addressing people on a first-name basis, using an English first name works well for educated, professional,

bicultural Chinese American immigrants. They feel perfectly at ease being called or calling fellow Chinese American acquaintances and friends by their English first names. Conversely, being called or calling casual acquaintances by their Chinese given names may not feel quite right, as the relationship may not quite warrant such familiarity and informality. The Chinese custom would be to add a title or a kinship term to address or be addressed by an acquaintance, which often seems too rigid and formal in America.

Some Chinese American immigrants adopt an English name and officially document the name change. Some go by their preferred English name without changing their name officially. In contrast to all of the meanings that are weighed when selecting a Chinese name, sound seems to be the main consideration when deciding on an English name. People often select an English name that sounds close to a Chinese given name. English names are usually chosen without checking the meaning and its origins; Biblical names may be selected without knowledge of their significance and without religious affiliation. American-born children usually are given an English name, and a Chinese name also may be given. Sometimes, the Chinese name is officially documented on the birth certificate as the middle name.

Other Relevant Information

The Chinese New Year

The Chinese New Year, also known as "The Spring Festival" to Chinese, is based on the lunar calendar. It is the first day of the first month of a lunar new year. The Chinese New Year usually falls between January 19 and February 20 in the solar (Gregorian) calendar. Each Chinese year is named after one of the 12 animals of the Chinese Zodiac. The same calendar has been in continuous use for more than 4,700 years; the Gregorian year 2002 was the Chinese lunar year 4700.

The most important holiday for all Chinese, the New Year is a time for family reunions, ancestor remembrance, the giving of thanks, and feasts with special foods and big celebrations. The old traditions of preparing for the New Year days in advance and celebrating the festival for 15 days with a grand finale of a Lantern Festival have been condensed and simplified to accommodate the demands of an industrial society. Among the major activities or celebrations associated with the New Year are: feasting with the family, ancestral worshiping, temple visiting, setting off firecrackers, having a dragon or lion parade, visiting relatives and friends, exchanging gifts, and giving "lucky money." Setting off firecrackers is intended to send off the old, welcome the new, and scare off evil spirits to ensure an auspicious new year. The parade of dragons, lions, and other folk dancers, accompanied by a loud orchestra of drums, gongs, cymbals, and ear-piercing firecrackers, is a display of joyous celebration and a blessing for a happy new year.

For Chinese children, celebrating the Chinese New Year is like celebrating Thanksgiving and Christmas at the same time. It is the most anticipated time of the year, even more so than one's own birthday. It is a time for special treats, visiting relatives, wearing new clothes, and receiving lucky money in a red envelope from parents and other elders.

In the United States, depending on the size of the Chinese American community, New Year celebrations vary from intense preparation that climaxes in the huge parade that closes down streets in San Francisco's Chinatown, to a few families getting together over the weekend to mark the New Year. Traditional celebrations are limited primarily to major cities with a larger Chinese American population. Nevertheless, hosting or attending a feast or two and giving "lucky money" to the youngsters are common practices. Family feasts often take place on weekends instead of on the official New Year's Eve or New Year's Day so that family members can enjoy the feast together. Some families perform ancestral worship before the feast by paying respect to departed ancestors, inviting and offering them the feast first, and asking for the ancestors' blessings. Special foods and treats with specific symbolic significance may still be served for the occasion, although on a simplified scale.

The Chinese New Year greeting phrase, *"Gung Hay Fat Choy,"* has become a well-known greeting for English speakers to use when wishing a Chinese American a happy new year. It is a Cantonese phrase. In the last few years, the Mandarin version of the phrase, *"Gong Xi Fa Cai"* (or *Gongxi Facai*), started to appear in greeting cards. The literal meaning is "Congratulations! Wish you strike it rich." The reason for offering congratulations springs from a legend about surviving the terror of a mythological monster that comes out at the end of the year to terrorize people and wreak havoc. *"Gung Hay Fat Choy"* (or *"Gong Xi Fa Cai"*) is only one of several popular greeting phrases.

As a matter of fact, some Chinese people prefer not to say this phrase, as it reflects a worldly obsession with money-making. Some people prefer to offer more spiritual wishes to reflect peace, auspiciousness, and success in other areas. One of the simple and safe alternatives for English speakers to say to a Mandarin speaker on Chinese New Year's day is *"Xinnian hao,"* which means "wishing you a happy new year" or "wishing you a good new year."

Cultural Considerations

Etiquette/Greetings. In accordance with the Confucian teaching of being humble, Chinese people generally are very understanding and excuse Americans for being unfamiliar with the Chinese customs and courtesies. Conversely, Chinese people also are quick to notice and appreciate a non-Chinese person's Chinese culture literacy in terms of proper protocol, procedures, and ways of addressing people.

When initiating greetings, proper recognition and respect for the vertical hierarchy and status is crucial. To follow the Confucian teaching of respecting elders, one should greet people in order of age. To show respect, it is appropriate to greet people with a slight bow and ask about their health, especially the elderly. A grandmother, who may not speak English or engage in the conversation and may actually prefer to stay in the background, may still acknowledge the politeness and good manners of a visitor and appreciate being greeted first. A smile with a slight bow and some simple niceties are appropriate. It is a good idea to be a bit formal, using appropriate titles such as Mr. or Mrs. with the surname. It is also a good idea to use common sense and be on the conservative side when interacting with the opposite gender. It is appropriate to nod and smile. Avoid initiating physical contact such as handshaking, kissing, or hugging, especially between a male and a female. Avoid winking, prolonged gazing, and close physical proximity between genders.

Eye Contact and Head Touching. There has been some misinformation regarding eye contact and head touching. Conference presenters often state that Chinese or Asian children are taught that eye contact is disrespectful and therefore they do not gaze into the eyes of elders or teachers. Hence, presenters may suggest that teachers not expect or demand an Asian student to keep eye contact with them. Such information is quite misleading, although it is true that many Chinese and Chinese American children may remorsefully lower their heads and stare at the floor when being disciplined. However, Chinese parents and teachers do expect children to attend to instructions and reprimands by keeping eye contact with them. Sometimes, children even may be chided for failing to show respect or attending to the speaker if they do not keep eye contact.

Teachers also are often advised not to touch Chinese American children's heads, because the head is the most sacred part of the body or because a child's spirits may be put in jeopardy if touched. This is not true with the Chinese. As a matter of fact, Chinese elders often gently touch or rub a youngster's head to show affection. Chinese teachers sometimes do the same, but not as often as elder relatives or government officials. Considering the social context in the United States, touching a student's head to show affection is certainly not encouraged. Nevertheless, head touching is not really a taboo.

Home Visiting, Gift Giving, Colors, and Numbers. Although not absolutely necessary, an appointment is appreciated, and becoming expected, before visiting Chinese Americans' home. Unless the host insists that you not do so, removing your shoes before entering is a polite gesture, especially if the host family members do not wear outside shoes in the house. Be prepared to hear the hostess's self-criticism of untidy housekeeping or the host's self-faulting of the modesty of the humble dwelling. During this exchange of niceties, the visitor is expected to offset the hosts' self-deprecation by paying compliments about the positive features of the house. However, avoid being overly specific when making such comments. A host may feel compelled to offer an object being admired to the guest as a gift. Food or drinks are usually offered and expected to be consumed, at least partially.

Whether one should bring a gift when visiting a home depends on many factors, as it does in the mainstream culture. When doing so, however, the subtlety of numbers and colors associated with gift giving needs to be heeded. Red and other warm and brightly colored wrapping is safe for all happy occasions. White is the color of mourning. When visiting a sick or recuperating friend, bring bright and colorful flowers and wear cheerful colors. White flowers and white outfits definitely are not appropriate for such an occasion. On the other hand, wearing bright colors to a subdued occasion is not appropriate, either.

In terms of numbers, even numbers are generally better than odd numbers, except four. Four, 14, 24, etc. are considered unlucky because the Chinese word for "four" sounds like the Chinese word for "death."

If you are not sure what gift to give, money in a red envelope, with or without a card, is gladly appreciated. Gifts, just like tea or drinks, should be offered and received with both hands. Standing up to offer or receive gifts or other drinks is also considered proper etiquette. Traditionally, gifts are not opened right away; they are opened later after the giver has left. Parents feel embarrassed and often chide their young children's bad manners and blame themselves for their poor upbringing when their young children display their impatience for opening their presents. Chinese Americans, however, may follow the mainstream practices of gift-giving with non-Chinese and the traditional practices with Chinese, especially if they are not American-born and still follow various aspects of the Chinese traditions.

Chapter 2
Family

Family Composition and Structure   **30**
    Extended Family and Other Cohabiting Practices   **30**
    Gender Value   **31**
    Kinships   **31**
    Marital Roles   **32**
Marital Relationships and Parental Responsibilities   **32**
Gender-Specific Roles of Family Members   **33**
Sibling Relations   **34**
Status and Hierarchy   **34**
Decision Making   **35**
Communication and Interaction Styles   **35**
    Parent-Child Communication and Interactions   **35**
    Spousal, In-Law, and Grandparent-Grandchild Communication   **36**
Relationships and Interactions With Clan and Friends   **37**
Summary and Implications   **37**
    Characteristics and Expectations of Chinese American Families   **37**
    Familial Discord   **38**
    Managing Familial Problems   **39**
    Counseling Considerations and Strategies   **39**

Family Composition and Structure

Extended Family and Other Cohabiting Practices

Traditionally, the Chinese family is patriarchal and patrilineal. A typical Chinese family consists of paternal grandparents, parents, children, and not-yet-married uncles and aunts. It is not unusual to see four generations living together in the same household. A typical three-generation family is still fairly common in most Chinese communities in Asia—as society evolves and employment patterns change, however, more and more families are becoming nuclear families. In Mainland China, the traditional "four generations under the same roof" has given way to "a family of three," because of the one-child-per-family policy.

In Chinese American families, the grandparents are more likely to live with their children and grandchildren instead of living in a separate dwelling, especially first-generation immigrants and refugees. Newcomer grandparents almost always live with their children and grandchildren, due to their insecurity associated with language and culture barriers and/or their children's child care needs. It is not unusual for parents to live with their married daughter and her family in America, even though this is not common in China, Taiwan, or other Chinese communities in Asia (where the older generation would live with a son). Some older folks do prefer to live alone, but usually not very far from their children and grandchildren. The older generation may choose to leave a son or daughter and the in-law alone to avoid friction caused by differences in personalities, life styles, and/or views on child rearing. The companionship, friendship, and activities provided by retirement communities or a senior housing complex also are incentives for seniors to live apart, especially in larger cities where they can find housing for Chinese speakers who are not proficient in English. Grandparents who live in suburbs with no other Chinese seniors around often feel extremely lonely when the younger generations are off at work or school.

In China, Taiwan, and sometimes in the United States, a not-yet-married adult child lives with his parents unless the job site is not within easy commuting distance from the family home. Young married couples in China and Taiwan generally stay with the husband's parents until they establish their own household, unless it is too far to commute, but this practice occurs less often in the United States. A young unmarried adult sibling sometimes stays with a married older sibling and his/her family, if they work in the same area and if the parental house is too far away from the job site to commute. These cohabiting practices often continue in the United States, and they reflect the interdependent nature of Chinese family dynamics. Mutual support and the comfort of being close to family override the need for privacy and independence, which is not heavily valued in the collectivist Chinese cultural context, although it is slowly seeping in as people become more acculturated.

Gender Value

The Chinese patriarchal, vertical family structure can be traced to the Confucian doctrine in which sons are more important and more valued because they continue the family line and carry on the family name. Sons are responsible not only for caring for parents when they become old, but also for providing proper burial and for worshiping their spirits when their bodies leave this world. Sons also act as caretakers of the spirits of other ancestors departed generations ago. Wandering and hungry spirits without a family to care for them in the yin world are as miserable and pitiful as homeless people in the yang world.

Traditionally, daughters are not considered permanent members of the family. Rather, they are "born facing out" and are raised for other families. With the number of children decreasing and public education prevailing, however, the gap of gender value has narrowed and favoritism of sons is becoming a thing of the past. Daughters have become much more valued, if not yet

of equal importance. Under the one-child-per-family policy, couples in Mainland China cherish their precious only child, whether male or female.

Daughters receive dowries when they are married, which may consist of cash, jewelry, furniture, appliances, household items, or even a car or house, depending on the family situation. Legally, daughters are entitled to equal inheritance along with sons; in practice, however, they usually do not inherit. Even if they do, they usually get smaller shares. Among Chinese Americans, the status of daughters is equal or almost equal to sons and, in most cases, daughters share a family inheritance with their brothers, especially in well-educated, professional families. In China, the first only-child generation is reaching adulthood and some are married. In many families, therefore, the daughter will eventually become the sole heir to her family's fortune.

Kinships

To the Chinese people, family is perceived through a system of relationships. While the extended network of kinship may appear complicated, the family structure is well defined along vertical and horizontal generational lines. Each person has a particular designation within the family, identifies himself or herself in relationship to other family members, and is referred to by corresponding honorific kinship terms. These kinship terms reflect the person's relative position within the family structure. A distinct kinship term is used for each of the two different kinds of brothers and sisters, the five different kinds of uncles and aunts, and the eight kinds of cousins.

Generation and age determine the hierarchy of authority and reverence. Younger generations are never allowed to call their senior family members by name alone. It is always "Uncle," "Aunt," or at least "Uncle So and So" or "Aunt So and So." Younger members of the same generation are taught to call their older siblings and cousins "Elder Brother" or "Elder Brother So and So." Chinese newcomers are appalled to hear younger Americans calling those of the senior generations by their first names. Also, first- and second-generation Chinese Americans often wonder exactly what relation one refers to when a general kinship term of "uncle" or "aunt" is used in the mainstream culture, as it is not clear to them.

Again, as society changes, such formality is relaxing; people are becoming more casual in addressing family members of the same generation, but remain formal with the senior generation. As China's one-child policy takes hold, sociologists have predicted that within a couple of generations, children in China will have a hard time understanding the different terms used in the Chinese language to distinguish among the different kinds of uncles and aunts and other relatives.

Marital Roles

Even today, eligible young men and women may be "set up" or "matched up" by relatives and friends. However, such matchmaking is done informally and in a more natural atmosphere, far from the old-fashioned matchmaking that was arranged by professional matchmakers. If a marriage does develop, it is almost always the fruition of a courtship that ensues after the initial set up and according to the mutual decision of the couple, not the families. Most young adults, however, find their own mates, with the man usually taking the initiative in the courtship.

After marriage, the husband is the head of the family, the rice winner, the protector, and the "minister of foreign affairs," representing the family as he interacts with the outside world. In fact, a formal term in Chinese for referring to one's own husband is "*waizi*," which literally means "the exterior one." On the other hand, "*neiren*" (the interior person) or "*neizi*" (the inside one) is a formal term for referring to one's own wife. She is the "minister of the interior," who is in charge of all internal affairs in her household domain. While the husband is the "minister of economics," producing income for the family, the wife is the "minister of finance," managing financial matters and controlling the wallet (Chan, 1998; Chen, 1988).

Although the roles the spouses play are counterbalancing and complementary to each other for the functioning of a household, the wife's status is not equal to her husband's. While it is traditional for the wife to submit to her husband, this subordinate status has undergone a transformation as the wife also produces income for the family. Still, the traditional marital roles remain largely the same, even in the United States. The husband may or may not take part in child-rearing duties and housework chores. In extended families with three generations, the grandparents usually assume the marital roles and responsibilities described above until they are ready to relinquish the roles and responsibilities to the second generation. In America, grandparents usually let their son and daughter-in-law take charge, mostly due to language barriers and their lack of acculturation.

Marital Relationships and Parental Responsibilities

Among Chinese families, the spousal relationship usually is considered secondary to the parent-child relationship (Lee, 1998). The connection and emotional attachment between a parent and child are considered stronger and more important than that between spouses (Chan, 1998; Huntsinger,

Huntsinger, Ching, & Lee, 2000). "Parental roles and responsibilities supersede the marital relationship. Parents are thus readily prepared to sacrifice personal needs in serving the interests of their children and in providing for the welfare and security of the family as a whole" (Chan, 1998, p. 297). "Quality time" between spouses is not a concept too many Chinese Americans parents, not to mention Chinese parents, know about. Chinese-American couples rarely hire a babysitter (Huntsinger et al., 2000). It is not unusual to see the mother stay behind to care for the children. The mother typically is very willing to sacrifice everything, including her social life, for the sake of her children, especially when they are very young. If a sitter is hired for an evening, it more likely is due to the need for both parents to attend a social obligation than simply a night out for the two adults to enjoy some leisure time alone.

Because of concerns for their children's welfare, parents, especially mothers, are not willing to divorce, even though the marriage at that point may be "in name only," with no real marital relations left. Exceptions are made for an extramarital affair, which is considered grounds for divorce. With divorce becoming more socially acceptable and less of a stigma in such situations, the wife is more willing to "stamp off" the marriage and let the mistress emerge as the official new wife. While the husband may remarry, the wife is more likely to remain single. Chinese society generally is cruel to divorced women, blaming them and deeming them less desirable as potential in-laws. In America, Chinese-American women who are divorced often find it easier to remarry or live with a partner who is not Chinese, thus distancing themselves from the Chinese community and removing themselves from virtually any interaction with other Chinese.

Child custody laws vary; with boys, it depends on the child's age and the number of male siblings and paternal cousins he has. A younger girl most likely will be placed in the mother's custody. A boy of the same age range may not "belong" to the mother, especially if there is a paternal grandmother to care for him or if he is the oldest or the only male grandson. In the United States, attitudes toward child custody may be more or less in line with the mainstream practice. Younger Chinese American children with divorced parents usually stay with the mother, while the father has visitation rights and/or custody of the children on weekends and holidays. Blended families do exist, but they are rare. Multiple marriages also exist, but are not common either in China, Taiwan, or in the United States.

Interestingly enough, while no comparative statistics are available, it is generally known among Chinese Americans that extramarital affairs or setting up another household to hide a mistress is much less common in America. It is believed that the "social climate" is different in the United States and that the temptations for men are not easily accessible. Two-parent Asian American households are definitely more prevalent. The 2000 Census showed that 81 percent of Chinese American families are two-parent families.

Gender-Specific Roles of Family Members

Male and female family members have gender-specific chores and responsibilities dictated by traditions. Men are responsible for doing chores that require bodily strength and for interacting with the outside world. Women are responsible for domestic chores and child care. Sons and daughters are assigned gender-specific chores similar to those of their parents. Chinese men frequently quote a proverbial saying, "Gentle-men stay away from the kitchen," as the excuse for not knowing anything about cooking. Although the gender-specific roles and responsibilities of Chinese family members have been long-standing traditions, communities in Hong Kong and Taiwan have experienced radical changes because of exposure to and contact with foreign cultures. Even in China, women work alongside men in the fields and have "held up half of the sky" since the establishment of the People's Republic. In America, Chinese American males and females find that the norms of American society make it easier for them to be liberated from old stereotypes. Most Chinese American women work, interact with outside people, and share decision-making responsibilities with their husbands. Men are slowly taking a small part of their share in household chores and child rearing.

Sibling Relations

The interdependent dynamics of the Chinese family structure dictate that an older sibling assumes the responsibility of caring for a younger sibling and being a role model (Tang & Park, 1999; Yee, Huang, & Lew, 1998). Just a generation ago, when most families had several children, it was not unusual for an older sister as young as 6 or 7 to carry a younger sibling on her back while playing. Nor was it unusual to see the eldest sister sacrifice her own education or marriage for her siblings' sake. She, then, was paid back with love, respect, and care by her siblings and their children during her old age.

With decreasing numbers of children in each family, such practices are rarely seen nowadays. However, a younger sibling is still taught to obey and respect older siblings. An elder sibling is expected to be a role model and often assumes the same responsibilities of a parent and is respected

as a parent. His or her spouse, then, also assumes the role and responsibility of a parent, and thus is duly respected. It is not uncommon for a younger sibling to live with a married or unmarried older sibling, if it makes the commute to work or school easier. In situations like these, the older sibling acts as a guardian or a caretaker.

While these practices of assuming the responsibilities of care-taking and performing the duties of a surrogate parent are rare in the United States, they may continue to a very limited extent. The traditional influence on the expectations of both the older and younger siblings is, nonetheless, evident. Some American teachers have noted the close relationships between Chinese siblings, the caring of an older sibling, and the obedience and respectfulness of a younger sibling. Despite a close relationship and the cultural expectations regarding sibling relations, however, Chinese siblings, just like any other siblings, are not immune from the universal problem of sibling rivalry.

Status and Hierarchy

Traditionally, generation, age, and gender are the determining factors of status and hierarchy within a family. Children are taught to obey and respect their elders. A Confucian family hierarchy assigns the highest authority and reverence to grand-parents, then proceeds to the father, mother, oldest brother, oldest sister, and then the youngest brother. A new daughter-in-law has hardly any status until the birth of a son, who then solidifies her position and elevates her status in the family. Her authority increases when she becomes the mother-in-law.

Within the Chinese American nuclear family structure, generation and age are still the major factors determining status and hierarchy, while gender plays a minor role, if any. While mindful of status and hierarchy, Chinese American families by and large have relaxed the rigid system of relationships and adopted a more egalitarian approach in decision-making processes and determining interpersonal relationships; nevertheless, they remain respectful of the older generations.

Decision Making

The collectivist orientation has a strong influence on the decision-making process. Contrary to those who follow an individualist orientation, a Chinese individual often seeks advice from one or several senior family members or makes a decision jointly with other family members. When making big decisions, younger adult siblings may be involved in the discussion. This approach to problem-solving and decision-making offers the individual support and helps the group reach a consensus. The determining factor of the decision-making process is the overall welfare of the family. It is not a forum in which to compete for acceptance or approval of one's own ideas or desires at the expense of the family; the welfare of the whole family comes before the individual's wishes.

When advice is asked, an answer is almost always given and taken directly and completely instead of perceived merely as a possible solution to consider. In the individualist culture, an individual is responsible for whatever consequences result from his or her own decision. In the Chinese culture, an individual is also accountable for the consequences of his own decision. However, support from the family usually is greater. The elders and other family members who supply the advice often feel responsible for the consequences and thus feel obliged to provide support. Chinese-Americans also practice this collective

approach to decision making, albeit influenced by the mainstream culture. There is also the issue of the availability of the elders in the United States; although parents may be available, other elders may not be (Chan, 1998; Matsuda, 1989).

Communication and Interaction Styles

Parent-Child Communication and Interactions

The concept of children's subordination to parents, in compliance with the Confucian family hierarchy, greatly affects parent-child communication and interactions. Traditionally, the communication pattern between parent and child is one-way: top-down, from parent to child, and often in the form of a command. The parent talks, makes a statement, gives directions, or asks a question, and the child listens and responds. Reticence in adult-child verbal interactions is valued. Children are often reminded that they have two ears but only one mouth; therefore, they are expected to listen more and speak less. Children are expected to speak when spoken to and respond when asked; otherwise, they are to use their ears and not their mouths.

The traditional father is cold, stoic, distant, and controlling. He maintains his solemn *"yan fu"* (strict father) image by not being very close to and warm with his children; the goal is to inspire his children's respect and fear. As Chan (1998) states, the father does not usually invite his children to confide in or share inner thoughts with him. The mother, on the other hand, is more nurturing, affectionate, and less controlling (Berndt, Cheung, Lau, Hau, & Lew, 1993; Ho, 1989). A child from a Chinese family will usually feel more comfortable approaching his mother to discuss things on his mind. The mother is also more sensitive in discerning the emotional and communication needs of the child and thus more likely to initiate verbal interaction with him. In some families, the mother acts as an intermediary between the father and the child.

The traditional father-child communication pattern, however, has slowly eroded somewhat. Education, western influences, and modernization have contributed to a change in father-child relation and communication patterns. The contemporary father, particularly an urban and educated one, has softened his image and seeks to be emotionally closer to his child; thus, he spends more quality time interacting with his child, including verbal interactions. The Chinese American father, in general, is more open when directly communicating with his child and less formal when interacting with his child. Nevertheless, some Chinese American fathers have yet to learn to relax and open up a two-way communication channel with their children. Exposure and acculturation to the mainstream practices certainly have persuaded most Chinese American fathers to break down the invisible wall between father and children.

Even so, although many Chinese American families are close, older children still may not communicate with their parents on more emotional levels. Instead, teenagers and college students often rely on their friends and siblings for such support. Older children communicate with their parents primarily about school issues and career plans. While the mother is more involved in their daily lives, when it comes to future plans and career decisions, Chinese American children tend to turn to their fathers for advice (Tseng, 1994). Conversely and interestingly, some educated mothers in China, Hong Kong, Taiwan, and America have traded such traditional roles with their husbands. These mothers, extremely concerned about the academic achievement and future success of their children, play the roles of strict disciplinarian, homework police, and grade pusher. Their husbands, then, take a more relaxed attitude.

Spousal, In-Law, and Grandparent-Grandchild Communication and Interactions

The communication and interaction styles between Chinese and Chinese American spouses can be characterized as mutually understood feelings that are not stated openly or verbally (Uba, 1994). As previously discussed (see the information on communication styles in Chapter 1), Chinese rely heavily on contextual and nonverbal cues in communication. Thus, the communication between Chinese husbands and wives is very indirect, implicit, and sometimes nonverbal. The message, however, is not hard for the receiver to infer. As discussed, the traditional Chinese value systems place a high value on discretion and refraining from a strong display of emotions. Chinese people usually do not openly display observable affection toward others. Public displays of physical contact between men and women are considered inappropriate; a husband and wife are expected to appear indifferent toward each other. Hence, interactions between spouses in public are limited (Chen, 1988).

The communication and interaction styles between in-laws are similar to those between spouses—indirect and highly contextual. Nonverbal cues are embedded and inferences are to be made by the receiver. By contrast, the communication and interaction styles between a grandparent and a grandchild are usually warm, and the bond is strong. When the grandchildren are young, the communication is direct and open and interaction is warm and casual. As the children get older, highly contextual communication and formal interaction styles become the norm.

Relationships and Interactions With Clan and Friends

As discussed in the sections on family composition and structure and decision-making, relationships and interactions with one's clan are very closely and tightly interrelated. In America, this relationship is even stronger. In Chinese communities across the United States, various "clan halls," "clan associations," and/or "family shrines" have sprung up to serve members of the same clans. Organizations also exist that serve people from the same geographic areas. In Chinese American communities, this support can be in many forms. Besides emotional and social support, it is not unusual to extend financial support to friends from the same region and members of the same clan.

Like any immigrant group, Chinese American newcomers seek out support from family or friends who arrived before them. Chinese immigrants and refugees, especially those with little or limited English proficiency, often rely on the comfort and security of "Chinatowns," where they feel more at home and where employment opportunities are more available for English learners. However, well-educated Chinese American professionals who are bilingual usually avoid living in ethnic enclaves, preferring to live in the suburbs with middle- and upper middle-class Americans. Merchants who operate successful businesses in the ethnic enclaves also typically prefer to live in the suburbs. Their newly arrived friends and relatives usually stay with them in their suburban residence, but may work in their businesses in the enclave.

In Chinese culture, more than hospitality is extended to the clan and to friends. Newcomers are welcomed as guests and as family members at the same time; they are treated as family members but without the accompanying responsibilities, although the guests usually do take on a certain share of the responsibilities. The less-acculturated Chinese Americans are more likely to have more relatives and friends stay with them longer in their house, even though their financial resources are comparatively limited. The more-acculturated Asians are more likely to have relatives and friends stay in the house for a shorter period of time. Members of the host family often cite issues of privacy and inconvenience as reasons for limiting their warm hospitality.

Summary and Implications

Characteristics and Expectations of Chinese American Families

The family forms the foundation of an individual's life. It is the basic unit in society. For Chinese and Chinese Americans, the family is more than a source of personal identity and emotional security. It is a hierarchy and a web of relations, as well as a reference group. The collectivist orientation of the Chinese family, shaped by Confucian teaching, exerts a strong influence over its members. This powerful force dictates the clearly defined roles and responsibilities of family members, underlines family harmony and solidarity, imposes the collective responsibility among kinship members, and advocates the virtue of sacrificing individual needs for the welfare and integrity of the family.

Chinese Americans, depending on the

level and extent of acculturation, hold on to these values and attitudes to varying degrees. Although this structured Chinese conceptualization of family is in direct conflict with the individualistic values of the American mainstream, many Chinese Americans manage to maneuver with ease in the social and familial contexts of the two cultures, while others encounter difficulty negotiating them.

Adhering to and performing the prescribed roles and responsibilities is a basic duty. Maintaining the integrity, harmony, and reputation of the family is of the utmost importance. Family members are brought up and urged to be mindful of the relations and the family hierarchy. It is expected that people will restrain feelings that may disrupt family harmony, as well as put familial welfare before personal interests. Socialized in this kind of cultural context, most Chinese Americans strive to confirm to the norm. They dutifully carry out their obligations, respectfully take care of their elders, willingly sacrifice for the good of the family, stoically control their impulses, sensitively strive to maintain familial harmony, and diligently endeavor to bring honor to the family.

By and large, most Chinese Americans succeed in complying with the culturally expected family obligations and maintain an intact and harmonious family. They interact appropriately in the bicultural, social, and familial contexts, making suitable adaptations to meet the needs of both cultures. When dealing with familial discord derived from cultural clashes, they are skillful in negotiating a compromise and striking a balance. They switch cultural codes easily, according to the circumstances and the needs, much in the way that someone who is bilingual can adjust to conversing in different languages.

Familial Discord

On the other hand, not all Chinese American families manage to achieve the desired familial harmony. Some of these failures are rooted in cultural conflicts between Chinese and mainstream expectations; others are not related to cultural differences. Family issues tend to fall into several categories. They include relationship problems with family members, marital discord, intergenerational conflicts, and clashes between familism and personal interests. The tradition of the nuclear family living arrangement in America greatly reduces relationship problems with family members, although the problems may still exist to a very limited extent. The most common relationship problems appear to center around power struggles between in-laws and tensions related to different styles of child-rearing. Marital problems and divorce often are viewed as failure by one or both partners to live up to the prescribed roles (Soo-Hoo, 1999). Because of the patriarchal and patrilineal focus of the Chinese family structure, considerable stigma is attributed to divorced women and, to a lesser extent, the children of divorced parents.

The parental perception of children as their own extension, coupled with the perception that a child's behavior reflects on the family, contribute to the belief that it is the parent's right and responsibility to influence and direct the child's choice of academic major, career, and marriage partner. These kinds of parenting practices, along with other parental demands and pressures, such as academic excellence and personal sacrifice, often strain parent-child relations and trigger intergenerational conflicts. Since a person's conduct affects not only one's own reputation but also that of the entire family, familial discord resulting from strained relationships not only subjects a person to a great deal of shame and guilt but also causes the entire family to lose face. So important is the reputation of the family that family problems tend to be handled within the family and disclosure to outsiders is suppressed (Sue, 1981). When irreconcilable problems arise, family members may believe that severing the relationship or disowning the child are the only solutions for preserving their family's reputation.

Managing Familial Problems

Regardless of the type of familial discord, Chinese and Chinese Americans generally take an indirect and subtle, rather than an open and straightforward, approach. Since much of the communication and interaction between and among family members is contextual and nonverbal, when tension arises, both sides involved expect the other side to pick up the nonverbal cues and react accordingly. This common strategy works well with minor problems if both sides are willing to make small concessions. Because some families rarely communicate at home and many families don't communicate on a more emotional level, underlying tensions often are not dealt with, but ignored with the hope that time will heal the rift. Time does take care of some problems. Unfortunately, many familial problems do not simply go away, particularly when the tension is not dealt with in a timely manner and is left to ferment.

As the tension intensifies, intervention becomes necessary. If sources of help for familial discord are unavailable or inappropriate within the family, Chinese Americans usually seek out help from relatives, trusted friends, or a respected teacher or elder. Family honor is so important that Chinese Americans resist or suppress admission of personal and familial problems and delay seeking counseling. Revealing the source of emotional problems is considered so embarrassing that Chinese Americans often develop somatic symptoms (Cheung, 1987; Sue & Sue, 1991).

Counseling Considerations and Strategies

Due to the extremely sparse literature regarding counseling of Chinese Americans and the highly specialized nature of counseling and family therapy, the following discussion on counseling Chinese Americans with familial issues will be very brief and general. There are some culture-specific considerations of which counselors and family therapists need to be aware. First, they should know that Chinese Americans are reluctant to reveal family problems because of the stigma and shame associated with having a familial problem and the culturally dictated way of coping with it through self-discipline and willpower. They may present personal and family problems in the guise of physical, educational, or vocational concerns (Sue & Sue, 1991). The delay in seeking help is sometimes compounded by poor verbal skills as well as the cultural preference for reticence. Counselors may need to employ the techniques of demonstration and role playing, and offer help with vocabulary (Chan, Lam, Wong, Leung, & Fang, 1988). Counselors and therapists also need to be sensitive to the clients' possible interpretation of overintrusion and attempts to undermine their psychological health. Generally speaking, Chinese American families prefer a structured, direct, logical, rational, and pragmatic counseling approach, with rapid diagnosis and prompt intervention (Huang, 1991; Leong & Gim-Chung, 1995; Sue & Sue, 1991). The reflective, unstructured, self-examining, and self-understanding approach most likely will result in the person terminating counseling sessions, perhaps after the initial visit.

Soo-Hoo (1999) suggests that family therapy treatment should focus specifically on changing interactions, and proposed that strategic therapy for working with Chinese American families should be: time-limited, pragmatic and practical, focused on solving specific problems, focused on changing interactions, focused on the present and the near future, focused on changing perceptions and ineffective behaviors, inclusive of the frame-of-references concept, and focused on developing behaviorally based solutions. Miller, Yang, and Chen (1997) suggest that the eight counseling strategies recommended by Sue and Sue (1991) for working with Asians also might be helpful for working with Taiwanese Americans. Huang (1991) also suggests some useful principles for working with Chinese Americans. Combining their suggestions, the following strategies are recommended:

- Avoid asking too many intrusive and indirect questions
- Educate and orient the client about the value of therapy, the role of the counselor, and the process of counseling; address the client's concern about shameful feelings regarding seeking counseling
- Focus on the specific problems and help develop client goals
- Be active and directive and convey a sense of authority
- Examine the environmental concerns
- Watch for intergenerational family conflicts
- Focus on solutions and limit the time frame for therapy
- Avoid confrontation.

Chapter 3
Child-Rearing Practices

How Children Are Perceived   **42**
    Parent-Child Relationship   **42**
    Parental Roles and Responsibilities   **42**
    The Child's Roles and Responsibilities   **43**
    Parent-Child Communication and Interactions   **44**
    Expectations of Children   **44**
    Priorities for Children   **45**
        Academic Achievement   **45**
        Cultural Preservation   **46**
        Etiquette   **46**
    Education and Schooling   **46**
    Perception of Birth Order and Gender   **47**
    Generation and Cultural Gaps   **48**
Caregiving   **49**
    Caregiving and Caregivers   **49**
    Grandparents and Caregiving   **49**
    Baby Carriers and Baby Carrying   **49**
Feeding/Food   **50**
    Breast-Feeding, Bottle-Feeding, and Weaning   **50**
    Baby Food   **50**
    Feeders   **51**
    Independent Feeding   **51**
    Food and Diet   **51**
    Mealtime Configuration and Family-Style Service   **52**
Toilet Training/Self-Help Skills   **53**
Sleeping Patterns   **53**
Parenting Attitudes and Practices   **54**
    The Concept of Training   **54**
    Chinese-Style Parenting Practices   **54**
    Parent-Child Conflicts Related to Parenting Practices   **55**
    Parenting in Infancy and Early Childhood   **55**
Child Discipline   **56**
    Conceptualization of Discipline   **56**
    Ages of Innocence and Understanding   **56**
    Parameters of Acceptable and Unacceptable Behaviors   **57**
    Disciplinarians   **57**
    Forms of Discipline   **57**
    Forms of Rewards   **58**
Implications for Educators and Other Professionals   **58**
    Cultural Influences   **58**
    Intra-Group Diversity   **59**
    Individual and Gender Differences   **60**
    Relationship and Credibility Building   **60**

How Children Are Perceived

Parent-Child Relationship

Chinese parents, like some other Asian parents, perceive their children not only as individuals but also as extensions of themselves (Chan, 1998; Tinloy, Tan, & Leung, 1988). Chinese mothers are very close to their children, both physically and emotionally. Babies used to be carried on their mother's back, and slept in the same bed or same room until they reached school age (or even later). When not being carried, babies are held or kept near a family member and are picked up immediately if they fuss (Chan, 1998; Chao, 1994; Huntsinger et al., 2000). Although these practices are not as prevalent as they used to be, babies are still carried and the co-sleeping arrangements are still pretty much the norm in China. In America, babies may sleep in the same room but are unlikely to be in the same bed. Youngsters follow their mother wherever she goes, and preschoolers sometimes fret and fuss, demanding to be carried around. Children usually are included in the social functions hosted by relatives and close friends when both parents attend. This practice also provides children with early exposure to, and participation in, social activities where they learn socially appropriate behaviors (Chan, 1998; Tang & Park, 1999).

Chinese mothers do not hire babysitters in order to attend social functions unless it is absolutely necessary. Mothers of very young children usually opt not to attend social functions with their husbands, unless hosted by a very close friend. In the United States, a Chinese American mother may occasionally hire a babysitter in order to attend a social function, but will rarely do so just to have some fun with her husband.

Parents' perceptions of their children as their own extension go beyond physical closeness. They feel responsible not only for their safety and well-being, but also for the behavior, achievement, and failures of their offspring. They may try to fulfill their own yet-to-be fulfilled aspirations via their children, and thus push or steer their children toward a certain path. They may take their children's achievement or failure so personally that they feel extremely proud or ashamed. As a result, the pressures and burdens on their children may be overwhelming.

Parental Roles and Responsibilities

In terms of parental roles and responsibilities, the guiding principle that governs the father-son relationship derives from one of the Confucian five cardinal relationships: *fu fu, zi zi* (He who is a father should behave like a father, he who is a son should behave like son). This philosophical view has been further expanded and interpreted to clearly define the parental responsibilities of proper child discipline and upbringing. *Yang bu jiao, fu zhi guo* (Raising a child while not teaching him is the fault of the father) has become a commonly known and cited saying to remind parents of their roles and responsibilities. As such, parents are expected to instill values and ethics, teach and model proper behaviors, and govern and discipline their children. They, then, are to be acknowledged or blamed for the outcome of their children's upbringing.

In recent decades, as academic achievement became linked directly to career success and prestige, parents have focused their roles and responsibilities on facilitating and promoting academic performance. Parents, especially middle-class parents and highly educated professionals, strongly believe that they play a significant role in their children's academic performance, and so they take the role as their child's teacher very seriously. They create a home environment conducive to learning and shape positive attitudes toward learning. They use a direct, formal, systematic, and structured intervention approach to ensure their children's success in schooling and learning.

Some Chinese and Chinese American parents teach their toddlers and preschoolers how to draw and print numerals and names. Often, parents introduce their children to counting and simple addition and subtraction, and provide private piano and/or violin lessons before or around the time they enter school (Huntsinger et al., 2000; Miller, Wiley, Fung, & Liang, 1997). Upon entering school, additional enrichment activities and supplementary lessons are carefully added and structured into the child's schedule to augment the child's education. Middle-class Chinese American families tend to choose such activities as Chinese school; after-school tutorial sessions; music and art lessons; scouting; and selected sports, such as tennis, swimming, and gymnastics (Chao, 1996a; Cheng, 1999; Huntsinger et al., 2000; Trueba, Cheng, & Ima, 1993).

In communities where there are concen- trated Chinese enclaves, such as the greater Los Angeles area, the San Francisco Bay Area, and the new Chinatown in Flushing, New York, after-school tutorial services to reinforce the three Rs and/or test preparation are doing a brisk business. Chinese newspapers in the United States carry a lot of advertisements about tutorial and test (PSAT, SAT I, SAT II, ACT) preparation programs. Ironically, most Chinese American children excel in school and do not need additional tutorial support. Parents feel ambivalent about enrolling children in these programs; many parents endured tremendous pressure themselves to pass a series of school and college entrance examinations and wish to spare their children similar trials. Most parents think these tutorial and test preparation programs are unnecessary, but they succumb to the pressure anyway. They worry their children will be at a disadvantage if others receive additional services and they do not. Believing not enough homework is assigned, some parents buy additional workbooks locally and from Hong Kong or Taiwan to reinforce what is taught at school, especially if no tutorial program is readily available or the cost is a concern. Nearly all Chinese or Chinese American parents, regardless of income level, willingly make what they believe to be the necessary investment and sacrifice, sometimes under extreme financial hardship, for the sake of their child's education (Chao, 1996b; Huntsinger & Jose, 1997; Huntsinger, Jose, & Larson, 1998; Huntsinger, Larson, Krieg, & Balsink, 1998; Pang, 1995).

The Child's Roles and Responsibilities

As discussed earlier, a child's role and responsibilities can be summed up in one word: *xiao*. *Xiao* is the ethical duty, a moral obligation, of being a child to one's own parents. *Xiao* exists on a continuum; on one end is basic duty and on the other is virtue. Children are obligated to behave as virtuously as possible; any child who fails to fulfill this role and responsibility is branded a moral and social criminal and condemned and despised by society. There is no real English translation for *xiao*. The idea of filial piety is somewhat close, but it does not quite encompass the totality of *xiao*. Nevertheless, for lack of a better term, filial piety has been accepted as the standard translation. It embodies all the roles, duties, obligations, responsibilities, and virtues of being an offspring to one's own parents. It includes, but is not limited to, being respectful and obedient to one's parents, being mindful of parental needs and wishes, fulfilling parental wishes, providing for the parents' physical and mental needs, performing ancestral worship, continuing the family lines, and bringing honor and glory to the family (Chen, 1988; Ho, 1994; Hsu, 1981; Shiang, 1984; Yao, 1979).

Since Chinese styles of interpersonal interactions are not physically or verbally open and demonstrative, fulfilling the duty of *xiao* involves thinking about the parents and anticipating and providing for parental desires rather than waiting for their requests (Shiang, 1984). *Xiao* is a lifelong process of repaying one's parents for their care, love, and dedication in birthing, raising, educating, and parenting. In the context of Chinese society, the concept of *xiao* is part of daily life and not hard to comprehend and practice. In America, Chinese American parents usually have a harder time conveying and transmitting the concept. Influenced by the mainstream culture, Chinese American children vary in understanding why some aspects of *xiao* are expected, resulting in compromises from both parents and children.

Parent-Child Communication and Interactions

In compliance with Confucian family hierarchy, the traditional communication pattern between parent and child is one-way, from parent to child. The traditional father is cold, stoic, and controlling, whereas the mother is more warm, affectionate, and nurturing. Generally speaking, the mother is more involved in the daily life of the child, but the child tends to consult the father for advice on future plans and career decisions. The contemporary father, especially the Chinese American father, however, is fairly open when directly communicating with his child and less formal when interacting with his child. For a more detailed discussion on parent-child communication and interaction, please refer to the Communication and Interaction Styles section of Chapter 2.

Expectations of Children

Extended literature research yields little empirical research published in English regarding Chinese or American Chinese parents' expectations of their children. It stands to reason that academic success and adherence to the codes of conduct would stand out as the basic expectations (Chao, 1996b; Kelley & Tseng, 1992; Zhang & Carrasquillo, 1995). A brief discussion will focus on these two aspects of parental expectations.

With the availability of public education, Chinese American children spend more than 12 years in school. Parents expect their children to put forth their best efforts to study hard so that they will excel academically. Upon a child's completion of secondary school, parents expect him or her to have acquired a marketable skill to obtain employment or, better yet, gained entrance to higher education and then even better employment. As a matter of fact, an overwhelming majority of Chinese American parents expect that their children will go to college, or even demand it. This expectation is interwoven in many daily interactions between the parent and child. It permeates all aspects of a child's growing up. This expectation usually is not explicitly indicated to the child but is understood from early on in a child's life.

Besides education or skill development, proper conduct is also universally expected. Parents expect the child to know what is expected of him or her and to behave accordingly. Researchers have found that Chinese parents demand and expect their children to obey authority figures, and to be aware of the sacrifices their parents have made for them and of the need to fulfill obligations (Zhang & Carrasquillo, 1995). Parents expect honor and glory, not shame or disgrace, to be brought upon the family. A study by Ho and Kang (1984) revealed that fathers and grandfathers in Hong Kong listed, in descending order, competence and achievement, moral character, sociability, and controlled temperament as the personal characteristics expected of their children and grandchildren.

Priorities for Children

Chinese educators advocate the holistic development of the child and emphasize the equal importance of all five categories of education: moral education, academic accomplishment, physical education, social skills, and arts. Schools and parents, on the other hand, do not follow or practice the same belief. Academic excellence has been narrowly identified as the top priority (Chen, 1989). Top "star" schools are known for academic excellence. Parents admire and envy others for having a child in one of those prestigious star schools. For Chinese American parents, cultural preservation is also a priority. Moreover, Chinese parents—both in the homelands and in the United States—are very concerned about the reputation associated with their children's behavior. Therefore, adherence to proper etiquette is stressed.

Academic Achievement. In China, Hong Kong, Taiwan, or the United States, academic achievement prominently stands out as the foremost concern for parents. In a cross-cultural comparison of Chinese and European mothers' beliefs about the role of parenting in preschool children's school success, Chao (1996b) concluded that Chinese American mothers wanted well-performing children, whereas European American mothers wanted well-rounded children. European American mothers did not want to stress academic achievement with their children; instead, they wanted to emphasize the importance of a more global and well-rounded style of learning in which the process of learning is more important than the outcome. Chinese American mothers, on the other hand, were very concerned with both the process and the outcome; process was included because it was related and vital to the outcome. Chinese Americans believed that acquisition of knowledge and mastery of skills were directly related to future career success. This is not to say that parents are not concerned about their child's morality, social skills, and artistic abilities, or that they would not like to see their child excel in all areas. Since no child can be talented and perfect in all areas, however, the focus has to be narrowed.

Academic achievement has become more and more of an obsession in the last few decades. It is quite common to hear conversations at social gatherings centering on the outstanding academic achievements of children of families or friends, such as gaining admission into a prestigious university or winning academic awards. The Confucian social strata, which elevates scholars to the top, certainly has been a driving force. The obsession of "pushing children through the narrow gate of college entrance exams," however, is a relatively new phenomenon. Since the introduction of public education decades ago, schooling has become within reach to the vast majority of citizens. Perceived as the means for upward mobility, education is the tangible ladder toward achieving a dream, either the child's own or a parent's interrupted or failed one.

Parents are willing to sacrifice nearly everything for their children's education (Huntsinger & Jose, 1997; Pang, 1995; Schneider & Lee, 1990; Tang & Park, 1999; Trueba et al., 1993; Wong, 1995; Zhang & Carrasquillo, 1995). People in the mainstream U.S. culture can easily relate to some of the sacrifices Chinese American parents make. It is understandable that Chinese parents would move to be near a better school or change their lifestyles to accommodate their child's education needs. Some decisions the Chinese make for their children's sake may seem a bit extreme or even outlandish, however. For example, some Americans may not comprehend why Chinese parents would mortgage their house to pay for college tuition or the tuition of a more prestigious university instead of a less expensive college. Neither can some American educators understand why parents would be willing to break up a family for the sake of the child's education. Since the mid 1970s in Hong Kong and Taiwan and since the 1990s in China, some well-to-do families voluntarily and purposefully split up so that one parent could move with a child or children to America for school, while the other parent remained behind to make money, which is sent to family members in the United States. Many of the so-called "parachute kids" or "junior foreign students" who started to appear in the classrooms in small numbers in the 1970s and in increasingly larger numbers in the 1980s and the 1990s fall into this category.

Cultural Preservation. Another priority that is very near and dear to the hearts of Chinese American parents is preserving and passing down their cultural heritage to their children. Many parents encourage (or even coerce) their children to attend Chinese school, which is more akin to a heritage language class. Detailed discussion on the Chinese heritage language school will follow in Chapter 4.

Etiquette. Besides academic achievement and cultural preservation, parents are also very concerned about the reputation associated with their children's behavior. The collectivist orientation of the Chinese culture stresses the importance of proper upbringing by parents. Therefore, a child's manner and behavior reflect on his parents and family, and the family's reputation is at stake if the child is perceived as bad mannered.

Education and Schooling

In terms of education, academic areas have greater priority for Chinese families than other school activities. Academic achievement is heavily emphasized. Parents do encourage children to participate in extracurricular activities, as long as they do not interfere with academic achievement. If such interference is perceived, however, they are quick to withdraw a child from the extracurricular activities.

Parents' aspirations often influence the child's education and schooling. Parents with a college education and above expect their children to earn at least a college degree, preferably a professional or an advanced degree. Parents without a college degree themselves also hope their child will graduate from college. The differences in expectations for sons and daughters in Chinese communities have narrowed; in the United States, no difference at all exists in many families.

While parents are slowly loosening up and letting their children make their own career choices, many parents are still pressuring their children to choose from among medicine, engineering, and science as their field of study. Job security, along with prestige and higher income, are the incentives for such preferences. In Chinese communities, differences in career aspirations for a daughter versus a son may still exist, to a limited extent. Traditional female careers may be encouraged in China, but that is hardly the case in the United States.

Among extracurricular activities, music appears to be the preference. Taking private piano or violin lessons is very common among children of middle-class families in Hong Kong and Taiwan. The trend is catching on among upper middle-class families in big cities in China. In parts of the United States with large Chinese communities, any private piano or violin teacher can attest to this preference, as the percentage of his or her students who are of Chinese descent is very high. Chinese American students also have a strong presence and high visibility in community youth orchestras and at piano or violin competitions, music teachers' conventions, and the Juilliard School of Music.

Although Chinese American children participate in soccer and other sports during elementary school, sports take a back seat by the time they reach high school. The reasons for emphasizing classical music instead of sports are many. First, Chinese parents perceive their children to be at a physical disadvantage compared to other races, as many are smaller in bone and muscle structure and in stature. Second, physical prowess is not highly regarded in the Chinese culture. Third, Chinese parents consider music more effort-dependent and less gift-dependent, compared to the visual arts or sports. In other words, music is considered an art form in which a child can excel if he applies himself. Fourth, music is associated with prestige and elitism in Chinese culture (i.e., a cultured person knows and appreciates music). Moreover, some parents themselves did not have the opportunity to learn music and do not want their child to miss out. Another important factor is that parents want to use music learning as a vehicle for cultivating discipline and building character. Confucianism believes in diligence and effort. Many parents point out that music lessons are not intended for training their child to be a concert pianist, but rather to instill the discipline of the work ethic.

In secondary schools, Chinese American students tend to participate more in orchestra, arts, the tennis team, the school newspaper, student government, and such academic-related extracurricular activities as academic "bowls," subject clubs, and math/science competitions (Huntsinger, Jose, Shutay, & Boelcke, 1997; Wong, 1995).

Perception of Birth Order and Gender

In China, the oldest son traditionally holds the highest status among the children, although sometimes the youngest son may be the favorite of the parents. Although daughters are not as highly regarded, the oldest and/or the youngest may hold a special position because of being the first-born or the baby of the family. Middle daughters usually are the least favored. As discussed in Chapter 2, the values attached to gender are distinct. Sons are expected to remain in the family, continue the family line, and carry the family name; thus, they are valued as more important. Sons are the future caretakers of the parents when they get old and the worshipers of their spirits when they die. Daughters are raised for other families. When they are married they become a member of their husband's family. Therefore, they are not considered permanent members of the family. As such, girls are less valued. However, with equal rights being advocated since the overturn of the last dynasty in 1911 and the decreasing number of children in each family, the value gap between genders has almost completely closed, especially in urban areas of Chinese communities in Asia. In Mainland China, since the imposition of the one-child policy, parents have no choice but to cherish their precious only child, be it a son or daughter.

In the United States, male and female children are equally valued, yet traditional expectations for boys and girls remain. A boy is encouraged to be muscular and dominant, whereas a girl is expected to be demure and submissive.

Generation and Cultural Gaps

Families in China, Hong Kong, and Taiwan, as well as in the United States, face the universal generation gap between young and old. The younger generation thinks the older generation is old-fashioned and too conservative, while the older generation thinks the younger generation is too cocky and immature. For parents in China, Hong Kong, and Taiwan, the generation gap is compounded by the cultural gap. Mass communication, media, and technology have a far-reaching impact on the younger generations worldwide. Chinese youth are not immune to the Western popular culture influences that

parents perceive as the biggest problem. In the United States, Chinese American parents lament that their children are losing touch with their cultural roots. Parental efforts to glorify the splendor of Chinese culture and impart its teachings often fall on deaf ears. The child who grows up in the mainstream and popular cultural context has little interest in and many problems relating to a distant past in which he or she does not want to play or take any part (Leung, 1997). The child's disinterest in or devaluing of the cultural heritage often widens the generation and cultural gaps and strains the familial relationship. Some families suffer severe cultural clashes and bitter generational estrangement, as parents remain adamant about imposing the Chinese values on the children and the children purposely despise or reject the Chinese culture.

Moreover, gaps between the generations exist in terms of values or expectations toward each other. As Amy Tan (1989) pointed out in the *Joy Luck Club*, Chinese parents expect their children to be both neurosurgeons and concert pianists. Iris Chang (2003), another bestselling author, gave even more detailed descriptions in *The Chinese in America* regarding the differences of generational expectations toward each other. She wrote that in the eyes of first-generation Taiwanese immigrant parents, a perfect child embodies the following qualities: scoring a perfect SAT of 1,600, attaining the skill level of a concert pianist or violinist, gaining admission and winning scholarships to an Ivy League college, and becoming a doctor or a college professor. The ABCs (American-Born Chinese), on the other hand, give the following definition of perfect parents: they don't impose dorky Chinese hairdos, disapprove of what their children wear, repeatedly hint at the importance of attending a prestigious college, or discuss their private matters publicly. Chinese American youths, no doubt, would concur with Chang. They likely would add a few more items to the list, such as not be so stingy, not be so restrictive about their social lives, not hint at their preference for a Chinese son- or daughter-in-law, not constantly "broadcast" their children's achievements, and not compare their children's grades with those of their relatives or friends.

Caregiving

Caregiving and Caregivers

Child caregiving responsibilities traditionally have fallen on the shoulders of the mother and her surrogates: the grandmother, aunt, or even an older sister. While the mother is the primary caregiver, other female elders in the extended household also help with the caregiving. With the disappearance of large, extended families, however, this kind of practice of multiple caregivers and shared caregiving has become a relic of the past.

The father and his surrogates—the grandfather and uncles—traditionally were rarely directly or physically involved in caring for the child. Nevertheless, fathers, especially urban and Chinese American fathers, are becoming more directly involved in the daily caregiving of their children. Grandfathers who, a generation ago, used only their mouths and eyes in supervising are learning to dirty their hands and physically care for their grandchildren, especially in the United States where they see how busy their children are and they need not worry about their image being ruined.

Grandparents and Caregiving

Busy parents greatly appreciate the caregiving provided by grandparents, as they often find work and child care responsibilities to be overwhelmingly demanding and exhausting. On the other hand, caregiving provided by grandparents can become a dilemma, due to different child-rearing styles. When it comes to child discipline, grandparents tend to be very doting and lenient instead of consistent and rational. Chinese grandparents, especially more traditional ones, have a tendency to interfere with parental caregiving practices, thus causing rifts between themselves and their adult children. It does not take long for a grandchild to learn how to manipulate the parents and grandparents, using the discipline issue to his or her advantage.

Baby Carriers and Baby Carrying

Babies used to be carried on their mother's back all day long, awake or asleep, so that the mother could go about doing her chores or conducting her business without worry-

ing about child care. A strip of cloth a few inches wide and several feet long, or a rectangular quilt with strips attached to the four corners, was used to strap the baby around the mother's back. Mothers or grandmothers used to embroider or decorate the baby carrier in anticipation of the baby's arrival. For toddlers or older children, a "piggyback ride" on the mother's back requires no carrier. Chinese toddlers enjoy being carried piggyback, and parents are often obliged to do so.

The majority of middle-class mothers in Chinese communities, however, have abandoned the carrying practice because it is considered old-fashioned. Some mothers worry that parting the baby's legs to strap the baby to the carrier's back may cause bowlegs or other minor deformities. Some progressive, urban, and educated Chinese and Chinese American mothers value the importance of bonding and want to maintain close physical contact with their babies, however, and have revitalized the carrying practice. These mothers often use a modern baby carrier bought from a store, carrying the baby either in the front or in the back. Poor mothers in rural Chinese communities in Asia may still carry their babies on their backs the traditional way with the traditional baby carrier, as they often have no choice but to do so in order to get chores done. An older sibling, especially an older sister, often helps with caregiving. It was quite common when families had many children for an older sibling to carry a younger child on her back with or without a baby carrier while playing with her peers (Yee et al., 1998). While most young adults in Chinese communities in Asia and in America have heard about the practice of baby carrying, unlike their parents, they did not experience it themselves when growing up.

Feeding/Food

Breast-Feeding, Bottle-Feeding, and Weaning

Before formula became available to Chinese mothers, babies were breast-fed on demand. Upper-class women did not nurse their own babies; instead, a wet nurse was hired (Lee, 1997b). Poor babies whose mothers did not have enough milk or could not nurse usually survived on rice water. Rice water (or rice soup) is the thin liquid made when rice is cooked with a large amount of water for a very long time. Eventually, the rice kernels break into such tiny soft particles that they are rendered almost invisible in the liquid. With the development and introduction of formula, many contemporary mothers in Chinese communities in Asia and the United States opt to bottle-feed their babies on a recommended rigid schedule instead of breast-feeding on demand. Misconceptions about the superior quality of formula and concern about losing one's figure, along with work demands and the convenience issue, were common reasons for the switch to formula. The switch to bottle-feeding, incidentally, also changes the weaning timetable. Traditionally, breast-feeding usually lasts a lot longer—until toddlerhood or even preschool age. Bottle-fed babies are usually weaned earlier, around the first birthday.

Baby Food

Watery, overcooked rice and the regular table food that family members eat are slowly added to supplement formula at about the same time that solid food is introduced to American babies. Toddlers, after their first birthday, mostly are fed the same table foods that family members eat. Before processed commercial baby food became readily available, babies were fed spoon-mashed solids. Or, the mother or another family member might chew the food first and then spoon-feed it to the baby. Both methods are still practiced, although they are not as common as they used to be. In American or in other Chinese communities in Asia, baby food grinders are commonly used nowadays to prepare homemade baby foods. Commercial baby foods also are used.

Feeders

Chinese mothers are generally over-involved in raising their children. This tendency, coupled with the collectivist orientation, decreases the emphasis on fostering a child's independence. Therefore, a baby is rarely given the opportunity to feed himself or herself. Occasionally, a baby may be given a bottle to hold onto, but finger food is not regularly given. If given, finger food is usually served as a snack rather than as part of a meal. A toddler or a preschooler is often spoon-fed. Independent feeding occurs later than is the mainstream American practice. The feeding of a toddler or a preschooler may occur prior to, during, or after the family's mealtime. Since some toddlers or preschoolers take a long time to finish a meal, some mothers will eat with the rest of the family first and then take their time feeding the child while doing other chores at the same time. The mother usually is the primary feeder; the father and other family members, such as the grandmother, also may help.

It is not unusual to see a toddler playing with a toy or running around while going back and forth to an adult for food during his feeding time. Chinese families do not sit these toddlers in a high chair during mealtime; instead, they allow children to run and play. Some children even run to their neighbors' homes, and so the mother has to track the child down. In the United States, most Chinese American families do use a high chair for the baby to sit next to the rest of the family during mealtime. Thus, the baby is included and treated more or less on an equal level. Using a high chair also allows parents to introduce finger foods, as they can be placed on the high chair tray. This provides an acceptable way for children to feed themselves and play with their food.

Independent Feeding

A Chinese mother typically uses a curved Chinese spoon or a western spoon to feed her baby or toddler. The youngster learns to self-feed with a spoon first and slowly makes the transition to chopsticks. One thing to note is that Chinese do not eat from a plate, but rather from a small rice bowl. The small bowl is brought close to the mouth so that the child can use the chopsticks to shovel food into her mouth—this is much easier than picking up food from the plate and bringing it to the mouth. Parents are tolerant of young children dropping their food onto the floor and making a mess when learning to self-feed.

Food and Diet

Drinks are not regularly served during mealtime, but soup is. Nowadays, milk is becoming part of the diet for younger children. Tea may be served as a drink before, during, or after the meal for adults. Soup is served at the same time and often consumed at the end of a meal instead of at the beginning. Soda, juice, or water is not put on the dinner table on a regular basis. Lunch and dinner follow the same routine, with rice being the staple food. In northern China, other grains, such as wheat, corn, millet, and sorghum, may replace rice as the staple food. Three to four dishes of meats, seafood, vegetables, and tofu are served with the rice, with one of the dishes being soup.

For special occasions, soda and juice are available to children, and adults may drink alcoholic beverages. Chinese women drink alcohol only to a very limited extent, while some Chinese men are heavy drinkers.

The food served for breakfast may be similar to lunch or dinner but simpler, with soupy rice instead of dry rice. Eggs, tofu, and preserved, pickled, or salty vegetables are often served, along with other simple dishes. City and town dwellers sometimes buy their breakfast on the run, just like people in the United States buying their breakfast from a drive-through window at a fast food place. The most common traditional choices are hot soy drinks, flat breads or steamed buns with fillings, and Chinese donuts. Chinese donuts are deep-fried, plain, foot-long bread with no glaze or fillings. Western-style sandwiches with eggs and ham and baked or steamed buns, with a variety of fillings, are also popular. In bigger cities in Chinese communities, Western-style breakfasts of toast, milk, and eggs are gaining popularity.

Fruit may be served at the end of lunch or dinner as a dessert or between meals as a snack, but not for breakfast. A dessert is only served after a feast or a banquet, but not on a regular basis. Since Chinese kitchens are not equipped with an oven, such cooking methods as baking, broiling, and roasting are not used for preparing Chinese dishes; foods are prepared on a stovetop (roasted meats and baked pastry are bought from stores or restaurants equipped with commercial ovens). Dairy products are not part of the diet for most Chinese, except milk for infants and small children and an occasional treat of ice cream, which was introduced from abroad.

Depending on the level of acculturation, the food Chinese Americans eat is en-riched and diversified to varying degrees. Common American and other ethnic foods, such as Italian and Mexican cuisine, are showing up on the dinner tables of Chinese American families. Breakfast and lunch are increasingly "Americanized" and simplified. A small number of Chinese Americans with a "Chinese stomach" prefer to take the leftover Chinese food from the night before to work. Chinese Americans differ from their counterparts in Asia in that they more often include dairy products in their diet, especially children and more acculturated adults.

Mealtime Configuration and Family-Style Service

During mealtimes, each family member fills his or her bowl of rice from the electric rice cooker that rests on the kitchen counter. Each person uses chopsticks to take other foods from the communal dishes placed in the center of the dining table. Except for a ladle or a big serving spoon for soup, serving spoons are not traditionally used, although some urban people are adopting the practice of providing serving utensils for communal use. This Chinese family style of dining does not involve passing the food around the table from one to the other. A soup bowl about the same size as a rice bowl or smaller is used for soup, or the rice bowl can double as a soup bowl. Curved Chinese spoons may be used for drinking soup, although some people drink the soup directly from the bowl. Parents usually prepare a bowl of rice with other food for younger children, while older children help themselves.

Giving thanks or saying grace is un-known to the majority of Chinese, except to Christian Chinese. Hoisting a cup of wine, tea, or other beverage for a toast is a common practice at a banquet. Family members usually gather for meals and start eating at the same time, but leave whenever they are finished. Leaving the table without asking to being excused is not considered bad manners. Mealtime is used as a time for parents (especially the father) to instill values (i.e., parents talk and children listen attentively). Children are not encouraged to talk during mealtime. With the transformation of the Chinese society, however, general conversation during mealtime has become more and more common. Mealtime has become a time for the parents and children to share the happenings of the day.

Toilet Training/ Self-Help Skills

Since Chinese mothers are close to their babies physically and emotionally, they are very involved in the caregiving process and procedures. Mothers are attuned to their babies' needs and to the cues associated with those needs. Therefore, Chinese mothers start toilet training their infants very early, as early as six months of age (Chung, 1997; Miller, Wiley, Fung, & Liang, 1997), although most mothers start training when the baby is around one year of age or about the time the baby starts walking. Mothers seem to know the timing of their infant's needs to eliminate by timing the intervals and by picking up on the baby's cues, which include facial expressions, behaviors, noises, or other nonverbal cues. The toilet training process is a gentle and gradual conditioning that takes a few months to accomplish (Huntsinger et al., 2000). The training involves frequently bringing the baby to and holding the baby over the toilet with legs parted while the mother encourages the baby to eliminate by imitating or initiating the noises the baby uses before eliminating (Chan, 1998; Chung, 1997; Huntsinger et al., 2000). Mothers

typically take the baby to the toilet when the baby first wakes up in the morning, before going out, upon returning from an outing, after a feeding, before bedtime, and following the noted time interval. Babies do wear diapers during training, mostly for protection only. Accidents do happen but not very often, and by the age of between 15 and 20 months, most babies are toilet trained. In the Chinese American home, babies are trained later, around age 2.

In some families, as soon as a toddler is toilet trained, he or she is regarded as independent, more so than American toddlers. The child is expected to be able to get dressed, although with some help with buttons or tying shoes. Some toddlers and preschoolers, on the other hand, may not acquire such self-help skills until much later, due to their mother's over-involvement. These types of mothers tend to do everything for their children and deprive their children of opportunities to learn basic self-help skills until later.

Sleeping Patterns

As described in the parent-child relationship section, Chinese mothers keep their babies in close physical proximity. While mothers today may not carry their children as much, they still keep their babies very close. In Chinese communities in Asia, the baby usually sleeps in the same bed with the parents and siblings. In the United States, a Chinese baby is less likely to sleep in the same bed, but is very likely to stay in the same room in a crib. Independent sleeping usually does not occur until school age in Chinese communities in Asia. If grandparents share the same household, a preschooler or a primary grade child may sleep in the same bed with a grandparent or grandparents in a separate room. In the United States, the practice of parents and children or grandparents and grandchildren sharing a bed is not common but still exists.

Chinese babies go to bed earlier, while bedtime for older children is usually later. Toddlers often want their mother to sleep with them. As soon as the little ones fall asleep, mothers often get up to finish the household chores or watch television. In some families, the mother does not accompany the children to bed first, and so the children often stay up, playing or watching television, until the parents' bedtime. As a result, the children have a hard time getting up early in the morning.

The mother's over-involvement with caregiving and the absence of quiet, quality time between husband and wife in the evening before bedtime may contribute to the child's dependence on the mother's companionship at bedtime. The Chinese practice of napping is pretty much the same as the American practice. During naptime, young children do not usually need their mother's companionship.

Parenting Attitudes and Practices

The Concept of Training

Studies examining Chinese parenting style and practices have suggested that Chinese parents are controlling, restrictive, and protective. From a Western point of view, Chinese parents may be characterized as authoritarian. From the Confucian perspective, Chinese parental control could be equated with parental concern, caring, love, involvement, and support (Chao, 1994; Gorman, 1998). Parental control is not intended for dominance, but rather for maintaining family harmony and fostering interdependence. Chinese parenting is embodied in the concept of training that

carries a very positive connotation in the Chinese cultural context, denoting "to love," "to care," "to govern," and "to teach" (Chao, 1993, 1996a).

Chinese-Style Parenting Practices

Although the very young are indulged and misbehaviors tolerated, due to the perception of children not yet being capable of understanding right from wrong, Confucian parenting principles stress early training on emotion regulation and impulse control. As soon as a child can walk and talk, he is trained to suppress and regulate his emotions and control his impulses. The goal is to make the child self-disciplined, hard working, and able to adhere to a standard of conduct. Upon reaching the age of understanding (around 5 or 6), the child is trained to understand the familial obligations and expected to excel academically in school (Ho, 1994; Kelley & Tseng, 1992; Tang & Park, 1999).

Parents do often shame, scold, and threaten as means of socialization and to raise the child's awareness of wrongdoing and its reflection on the family (Chung, 1997; Lee, 1997a; Pikcunas, 1986; Tang & Park, 1999). It should be noted that the Chinese operate with a self-critical rather than a self-affirming framework, and that Chinese parents believe that children need to learn to take criticism at an early age (Huntsinger et al., 2000; Miller et al., 1997). Additionally, parents use didactic narratives of exemplary folk stories, personal storytelling, interactions with siblings and peers, and exposure to role models to instill values and impart morality (Miller et al., 1997).

Positive reinforcement may be expressed through the absence of scolding, silence, and a slight smile. Acknowledgement of achievement is very subtle and implicit.

Overt or direct praise is rare, especially toward older children. Affection is often expressed via food. Thus, the Chinese framework of a strong, controlling, and aggressive parental role is closer to the authoritative style practiced by the mainstream (Chao, 1993, 1994; Chiu, 1987; Lin & Fu, 1990). The findings of a more recent study by Chen and Luster (1999) that involved 463 mothers also showed that the authoritative pattern was predominant among mothers in Taiwan.

Understandably, Chinese American parents modify their parenting attitudes and practices as they acculturate in the mainstream culture. Yao (1981, cited in Zhang & Carrasquillo, 1995) found that Chinese American parents assume less authority as they adopt American methods of child rearing. Nonetheless, the passive style of giving positive reinforcement and limited expression of affection is hard for children to understand. Elementary school-age Chinese American children often complain that their parents are not as sweet as their friends' parents. They know that their parents love them and are proud of them, but wonder why their parents do not openly express their affection as much as their friends' parents do. They can't understand why their parents rarely model the polite manners expected of them.

Parent-Child Conflicts Related to Parenting Practices

Parents' controlling behavior is perceived by adults as necessary and positive for the good of the children. The children, on the other hand, view it differently. First- and second-generation Chinese American youths reported later-age expectations than white Americans for behavior autonomy, such as staying out late, choosing friends, and making their own decisions (Feldman &

Rosenthal, 1990). Adolescents especially resent the lack of autonomy, respect, and trust. These differences in perception concerning parenting often cause conflicts between parents and adolescents or their young adult children (Lau, Lew, Hau, Cheung, & Berndt, 1990; Lee, 1997a; Lee & Zhan, 1998). The most common conflicts seem to center around academic issues such as homework, grades, and college major/career choice, as well as dating/marriage issues (Lee, 1997; Yau & Smetana, 1996). Such intergenerational conflicts over parenting, compounded by the cultural gaps in the United States, are especially challenging for Chinese American families.

One study reported that mothers generally are perceived as warmer, less restrictive, and less controlling than fathers are (Berndt et al., 1993). However, many observers indicate that contemporary and achievement-minded mothers can be warm and nurturing, yet still be controlling and restrictive. They are so concerned with their children's success that they guide their children with a very firm grip.

Parenting in Infancy and Early Childhood

Chinese parenting practices typically do not emphasize such socialization skills as verbal interactions and cognitive stimulation in infancy. While the mother keeps close physical and emotional proximity to the baby, she makes little effort to stimulate vocalization, except for casual and occasional verbalization, as compared to European-American practices (Chan, 1998). Even immigrant Chinese mothers reported less nurturance and responsiveness than Caucasian American mothers, which suggests that Chinese mothers focus on taking care of their child's physical, rather than psychological, needs (Hsu, 1985; Kelley & Tseng,

1992; Smith & Freedman, 1983). The traditional practice of carrying the baby on the mother's back may impede critical face-to-face interactions and it also may limit the infant's opportunities for exploration and "floor time." Chinese houses are not carpeted or child-proofed, and therefore free exploration, especially on the floor, is extremely limited. Infants and toddlers are carried, held in the lap, and put in a crib or walker. Parents do not routinely sit on the floor or lower down to the child's physical level to play with the child. Furthermore, parents' over-involvement and over-protectiveness result in few opportunities for developing autonomy and initiative in infancy and early childhood (Chung, 1997).

However, with the passage of time and with families having only one child or two children, the contemporary generation of urban and educated mothers seems to engage older toddlers and preschoolers more in activities associated with school readiness and academic success. Direct and intentional teaching of language, songs and nursery rhymes, drawing, handwriting, or counting, as well as explicit, elaborative, event-specific literacy-related activities, has been observed and reported in the United States, Taiwan, and China (Huntsinger et al., 2000; Huntsinger, Jose, & Ching, 1994; Huntsinger, Schoeneman, & Ching, 1994; Miller et al., 1997; Steward & Steward, 1974; Wang, Bernas, & Eberhard, 2002). Better-educated parents also tend to favor encouraging initiative and autonomy.

Child Discipline

Conceptualization of Discipline

The Chinese believe that the development of positive character requires proper training and strict discipline. Chinese parents hold high expectations for their children's con-

duct and believe that they would be remiss as parents if they didn't provide the proper upbringing and discipline (*yang bu jiao, fu zhi guo*). The expression "Spare the rod and spoil the child" has a nearly identical Chinese equivalent (*bu da bu cheng qi*). The Chinese saying, "It's the child who's getting spanked on his body, but it's the mother who hurts in her heart" (*da zai er shen, tong zai niang xin*), clearly delineates that severe physical punishment for transgressions is not child abuse, but expression of parental love and responsibility. "The deeper the love, the greater the correction" (*ai zhi shen, ze zhi qie*), another Chinese idiom, is often quoted by adults to explain and justify a punishment to an older child.

Thus, the conceptualization of child discipline illustrates the basis of the restrictive and controlling style of Chinese parenting. Limited available literature has suggested that Chinese parents utilize scolding, shaming, and punishing as means to train children (Chan, 1998; Chung, 1997; Kelly & Tseng, 1992; Lee, 1996; Suzuki, 1980; Tang & Park, 1999; Tinloy, Tan, & Leung, 1988; Wu, 1985).

Ages of Innocence and Understanding

Chinese people conceptualize early childhood moral development in two distinct stages: the age of innocence and the age of understanding. During infancy and the preschool years, the child is viewed as functioning in the age of innocence and ignorance, not capable of understanding right from wrong. This parental conception of very young children's capabilities is the basis for not imposing discipline and holding them accountable for any wrongdoings at that stage. Thus, Chinese parents tend to be very tolerant, lenient, and indulgent toward infants, toddlers, and preschoolers, and eager to gratify their needs. When the child is about to enter school, however, parental expectations change abruptly and strict discipline is imposed, because the child is viewed as having reached the age of understanding and therefore being capable of distinguishing right from wrong (Bond & Hwang, 1986; Ho, 1986, 1989; Ho & Kang, 1984; Stevenson, Chen, & Lee, 1992; Suzuki, 1980; Tang & Park, 1999; Wolf, 1970).

Parameters of Acceptable and Unacceptable Behaviors

Acceptable behaviors are those that reflect adherence to specific roles, relationships, duties, obligations, and codes of conduct. Failure to fulfill one's roles and responsibilities and maintain the family honor, violating the codes of conduct, or displaying undesirable behaviors, such as disobedience toward parents and aggression toward siblings, are unacceptable and subject to punishment.

Disciplinarians

Traditionally, the mother is the main disciplinarian for daily problems, especially in matters involving siblings. The mother usually delegates the father to carry out the punishment for major offenses or serious misbehaviors, although the mother also has a role in that process. She verbally disciplines the offender before the punishment is meted out, and often takes part in imposing more verbal admonishments during the actual execution of the punishment. Sometimes the mother serves as a monitor to ensure that the child is not physically punished too severely by an emotionally irate father. At other times the mother pleads for mercy or serves as a rescuer for the child. Grandparents and other adult relatives, if available, also may plead their case for the offender.

Grandparents can pose a problem for parents, sometimes emotionally interfering instead of facilitating the discipline in a rational manner. Some even go to the extreme of criticizing the parents while protecting or rescuing the child. The child, then, takes advantage of the inconsistent messages and manipulates the parents and grandparents. Grandparents and other adults do monitor children's behavior, but usually do not implement physical forms of punishment. After verbally disciplining the offender, they usually report the misbehavior to the mother or the father and let the parent carry out the primary disciplinarian measures.

Forms of Discipline

Disciplining a child takes three forms: verbal reprimand, physical punishment, and repenting time-out. These three forms usually are used in combination. Verbal reprimand is the most commonly used tactic, and includes harsh scolding, yelling, criticizing, name-calling, shaming, and threatening (Bond & Hwang, 1986; Chan, 1998; Ho & Kang, 1984; Kelley & Tseng, 1992; Suzuki, 1980; Tinloy et al., 1988; Wu, 1985). A trivial misbehavior may only be responded to with a verbal admonishment. For a more serious infraction, a tongue-lashing usually is followed by placing the child in a repenting time-out that may take the form of facing the wall or kneeling down for a long period of time. Sometimes, the offender is sent to face or kneel down in front of the ancestral tablet to repent. In addition, threatening (or actual) withdrawal of love, banishment, and/or isolation of the child from the family household or social life may be imposed.

Physical punishment includes twisting the ears, arms, or legs; slapping the cheek; rapping knuckles on the head; hitting the palms with a ruler or stick; using a belt to whip the legs or buttocks; and paddling with a stick on the legs, arms, and buttocks. The mother usually employs more of the twisting, slapping, and palm hitting, while the father uses the more severe forms of punishment, such as whipping and paddling. Corporal punishment is rarely executed alone; it is almost always accompanied by harsh verbal reprimands.

After the physical punishment, it is not unusual to have additional repenting time-out imposed. Chinese Americans, if acculturated, are aware of the prohibition against physical punishment of children in the United States. Newcomers, unfamiliar with the law of the land, sometimes learn about the prohibition the hard way by being reported, arrested, and prosecuted for child abuse.

Forms of Rewards

Chinese parents are not verbally interactive or physically demonstrative with their children. Because of their high expectations for their children, parents deem acknowledgement of the child's noteworthy success to be unnecessary and thus it is limited or nonexistent in many families (Cheng, 1999; Tinloy et al., 1988). Modern and urban parents of younger children may offer contingent praise and overt material rewards. More traditional parents, and parents of older children, may not verbally or behaviorally express their pride in their children's achievement. Sometimes, these parents manifest their acknowledgment of a child's accomplishment indirectly or in the form of exhortations to strive for even more (or a higher level of) achievement (Chan, 1998; Tang & Park, 1999). Sometimes rewards are manifested in a subtle way without verbal or explicit acknowledgement. A favorite dish, a special long-awaited item, special privileges, and a special gift are examples of parental acknowledgment and rewards. The honor of being asked to perform a special task is another form of reward. When these rewards are bestowed upon the receiver, he or she is fully aware of the significance, even though explicit acknowledgement is absent.

Although traditional parents rarely tell their children that they are proud of them, they sometimes verbalize their pride in their children's accomplishments to extended family members and close family friends. Overhearing comments like this means a great deal to a child. Emotional rewards of this type provide the child with enormous acknowledgement, bolstering pride and fueling the intrinsic motivation to work harder. In sum, success or accomplishment is expected in the traditional sense. Rewards come in varied forms, depending on the age of the child and the extent to which the parents adhere to the tradition.

Implications for Educators and Other Professionals

Teachers, counselors, therapists, child protective agency workers, and other service providers should be aware that some culture-specific factors exist that influence parental perceptions regarding professional intervention and services, specifically concerning child-rearing issues. Cultural influences, intra-group diversity, individual and gender differences, and relationship and credibility building are crucial factors to keep in mind.

Cultural Influences

Chinese Americans have long-standing cultural traditions. As such, their cultural roots run very deep, their cultural influences are very strong, and their traditions are well-integrated into all aspects of their lives. Many Chinese Americans are oblivious to the fact that their cultural influences profoundly permeate their communication patterns, ways of thinking, and outlook on life. In terms of child-rearing practices, both the literature (Ho, 1989; Kelley & Tseng, 1992; Siu, 1992a) and personal observations reveal that even American-born Chinese parents retain some traditional Chinese parenting values and practices.

To varying degrees, these traditional influences are evident in Chinese American parents' perceptions of, expectations for, and priorities for children; parenting attitudes; parent-child interaction styles; parenting practices; and conceptualization and forms of discipline. Moreover, Chinese styles of parenting practices are surprisingly consistent in China, Hong Kong, Taiwan, and North America (Ho, 1989; Siu, 1992a). This finding is significantly indicative of the strong cultural influences, considering the tremendous regional and political-social differences.

In sum, Chinese parents, either in the United States or in Asia, tend to be more controlling and protective, emphasize obedience, value and expect higher academic achievement, believe more in effort and less in innate ability, and are less satisfied with a child's achievement.

Overall, the strong and long-lasting traditional influences imply that changing child-rearing views and practices for Chinese Americans won't be easy. For Chinese American parents, compromising or negotiating between the Chinese traditional cultures and the mainstream cultures is more than soul searching. It will take time, and the acculturation process is a lengthy one. When working with Chinese American parents who are in the process of negotiating between cultures, professionals need to be genuinely understanding, sensitive, empathic, and patient.

Intra-Group Diversity

While the traditions exert widespread and deep-rooted influences, educators and professionals also must keep in mind the tremendous intra-group diversity among Chinese Americans in terms of differences in acculturation, education level, socioeconomic status, and socialization patterns. Some Chinese Americans are fifth- or sixth-generation American-born Chinese Americans. Some are fresh off the plane. Some Chinese Americans are the so-called "uptown" Chinese, who tend to be upper-middle class, highly educated professionals living in the suburbs. Some are the so-called "downtown" Chinese, who tend to be new immigrants with less education, little or no transferable skills and limited English proficiency. They live in inner cities or Chinatowns and work at low-paying, manual jobs. Among the newcomers, some are fortunate to have a network of support and resources. Some do not.

Depending on the community the family settles in upon arrival, the socialization pattern differs. A family that settles in a small town in the Midwest with few other Chinese families around is likely to have different interaction and socialization patterns with the mainstream culture than a family settling in the San Francisco Bay area. Understandably, immigrants with a rural background and lower socio-economic status, less education and limited financial resources, speaking limited English, and living in an inner-city Chinese enclave are more likely to adhere to the traditional child-rearing values and practices. For them, negotiating between both cultures and acculturating to the mainstream practices will take longer.

On the other hand, bilingual and bicultural services related to child-rearing interventions and services are more likely to be available in the immediate community. Professionals may want to tap into the resources available and collaborate with the professionals or paraprofessionals in the Chinese American communities to provide services that are culturally and linguistically appropriate.

Individual and Gender Differences

It is always prudent to heed individual differences in addition to intra-group differences. Like any ethnic group, Chinese Americans come in all sizes and shapes. It is always a good idea to know, regard, and treat each and every Chinese American as an individual first, culture-specific background notwithstanding. Professionals must remember that some Chinese Americans are more open-minded, easygoing, flexible, and willing to adapt and adopt new values and adjust to new child-rearing practices, while others are not.

Most Chinese Americans view authority and professionals with respect and are eager to follow along and compromise. However, some may view professionals with uneasiness or even suspicion. For example, a parent with a rural background or limited education may not have any idea about counseling, therapy, or intervention. Due to work schedules, lack of child care, limited English proficiency, or unfamiliarity with or misconception about intervention, the parent may be unavailable to meet with teachers or become involved at school. When interacting with authority figures, Chinese American parents may appear extremely humble or to have low self-esteem.

While seemingly uncaring and unconcerned, the parents are, nonetheless, very concerned about their children's futures and hold high aspirations for them. Professionals' awareness of and sensitivity to indi-

vidual differences will go a long way toward establishing relationships, building trust, and ensuring full cooperation.

Gender difference also is worth mentioning. Although it may appear to be a generalization, Chinese men are less likely to change their perceptions, attitudes, and practices concerning child rearing. Chinese women, at least ostensibly, can be more pleasant to work with and more willing to compromise. Chinese American mothers, especially nowadays, do have more clout and play a major role in the decision-making process concerning child rearing. Professionals may want to approach the mother if they can't seem to get the father to listen. Of course, they need to proceed with caution, common sense, and professionalism.

Relationship and Credibility Building

Finally, professionals might want to remember that interventions and services begin by building a relationship and credibility. As Lee (1997b) points out, forming a social and cultural connection with the family at the beginning, establishing credibility, and building trust are especially effective strategies for working with Chinese American families. It might be worthwhile for educators and service providers to be flexible, form social relationships with the families, and forge a cultural connection. In addition to being a teacher or a therapist, one may assume the role of friend, advocate, cultural facilitator, or mediator. The Chinese tradition of respecting well-educated people implies that it is critical to establish credibility. Credibility or professional expertise can be established by radiating confidence and maturity, demonstrating knowledge about Chinese culture and community resources, demonstrating skills in cross-cultural communication, displaying academic credentials, and offering concrete and effective solutions to problems (Lee, 1997b). Such strategies as knowing the Chinese style of high-context communication patterns, fine-tuning listening skills, interpreting nonverbal cues and body language, tactfully eliciting information, and asking the right questions at the right time are helpful in not only facilitating communication but also building trust.

Chapter 4
Education

Attitudes Toward Education   **64**

Perception of Parental Role in the Child's Schooling   **65**

Parental Perception of the Teacher's and School's Roles and Responsibilities   **65**

Education System in the Homelands   **66**

Similarities and Differences Between Chinese and American Schools   **67**

Differences in Classroom Interactions   **69**

Learning Styles of Chinese Students   **71**

Linguistic Issues   **72**

Academic Success and Difficulty   **73**

    Polarized Academic Performances   **73**

    Theories of Academic Success   **73**

    Cultural Factors Related to Academic Performance   **74**

        Parental Attitudes   **74**

        Student Attitudes   **75**

        Effort   **75**

    Academic Difficulties   **76**

    Chinese American Students at Risk   **76**

        Poverty and Distractions From Academic Focus   **76**

        Lack of Parental Support and Supervision   **76**

        Risk Factors in School and Societal Contexts   **77**

Parental Pressure and Academic Stress   **77**

Parental Involvement and Interactions With Teachers and the School   **78**

Heritage Language School   **79**

Parental Perceptions of Extracurricular Activities   **81**

Implications and Recommendations   **81**

    Administration and Leadership   **81**

        Cultural Literacy and Staff Development   **82**

        Community Outreach and Involvement   **82**

        A Bilingual and Bicultural Support System   **83**

        Parent Leadership Empowerment   **84**

    Classroom Interactions   **84**

        Student-Teacher Relationship and Interactions   **84**

        Classroom Teaching-Learning Interactions   **85**

        Accommodating Learning Styles   **85**

    Counseling   **86**

        Indirect Service Approach   **86**

        Culturally Appropriate and Responsive Counseling   **86**

    Partnership-Building With Parents   **87**

        Cultural Literacy and Self-Reflection   **87**

        A Support System To Build Relationships   **87**

        Language and Culture Barriers   **87**

        Personal Touches and Connections   **88**

Attitudes Toward Education

Education has always been highly valued in China, where scholars traditionally have perched at the top of the social strata. The rich and famous may be envied, but they are not respected unless they are also well-educated. It is the scholars who command admiration and veneration. As such, teaching, although not a well-paid profession, has always been considered a noble calling. A common saying, "Compared to scholarly pursuits, everything is lowly," reinforces the tradition and reminds young people of scholarly aspiration. On a pragmatic level, education is the ladder for upward mobility. Wealth and power were, and may still be, the material rewards of assiduous study. The moral of diligent study paying off infuses folklore and drama, idolizing poor young men who ascended to high positions by studying diligently. An adage, "A gold mansion and a beautiful girl whose face is as fair as a piece of jade await you inside your books," is frequently quoted to motivate and encourage devotion to scholarly pursuit.

This tradition must have been ingrained into the hearts and minds of the Chinese people. As discussed in Priorities for Children (in Chapter 3), Chinese parents and Chinese society as a whole equate children's academic achievement with parental success. Before the definitions of the "model mother" were diversified 10 to 15 years ago, all mothers hailed as the "model mothers" on Mother's Day in Taiwan were mothers whose children had achieved extraordinary academic accomplishments. Within this kind of social context, it is not surprising to find research reports confirming that Chinese parents, compared to American parents, put more value on education, shape positive attitudes toward learning, and have higher expectations for their children (Chen & Uttal, 1988; Fong, 2002; Lee, 1995; Stevenson, Lee, & Stigler, 1986; Wong, 1995; Yee et al., 1998). Parents are willing to sacrifice nearly everything for their children's educational pursuits (Huntsinger & Jose, 1997; Lee, 1995; Pang, 1995; Schneider & Lee, 1990; Trueba et al., 1993; Wong, 1995; Zhang & Carrasquillo, 1995).

In recent decades, with the increasing availability of public education, most parents have been obsessed with devoting all their energy and resources to helping their children gain access to higher education. Children, in the meantime, are socialized to achieve academically and have been reported to like school in general more than their American counterparts. Elementary school children in China were reported to engage more in academic activities, think more about things related to schoolwork on their way to school, and mention more education-related wishes than American children did (Chen, 1989). Ho (1994) also reported that students in China and Hong Kong were significantly more achievement-oriented than European students, and that the majority of the secondary students in Hong Kong aspired to higher education. Limited research on Chinese American high school students shows similar results. Wong (1995) reported that 88 percent of Chinese American high school students (vs. 62 percent of white students) indicated that they would be disappointed if they did not graduate from college, and 44 percent of Chinese American students (vs. 21 percent of white students) indicated an expectation to attain some postgraduate degree. Additionally, Chinese American high school students were reported to strive for admission to more selective colleges and universities (Huntsinger et al., 1997).

This attitude toward education, although admirable, has its shortcomings. Often, the obsessive focus on academics is at the expense of other learning. Parents want their children to devote time to studying so much that children do not have time or opportunity to learn very basic self-help skills, such as doing laundry, simple cooking, or household chores. A young adult may function at a very high cognitive level, but may not have common sense dealing with simple, real-life situations.

Perception of Parental Role in the Child's Schooling

With the traditional respect toward scholars and learning, as well as the preconception of academic achievement being linked directly to career success and prestige, parents have focused their roles and responsibilities on facilitating and promoting academic performance. Parents, especially middle-class parents and highly educated professionals, strongly believe that they play a significant role in their children's academic performance and take the role of teacher very seriously. They create an environment conducive to learning and shape positive attitudes toward learning. They use a direct, formal, systematic, and structured intervention approach to ensure their children's academic success. After-school enrichment activities and supplementary learning, such as music lessons and tutorial sessions, are carefully added and structured into the child's schedule to augment the child's education and enhance academic performance. Furthermore, nearly all Chinese or Chinese American parents, regardless of income level, willingly make the necessary investment and sacrifices, sometime under extreme financial hardship, for the sake of their child's education (Chao, 1996b; Huntsinger & Jose, 1997; Huntsinger, Jose, & Larson, 1998; Huntsinger, Larson, et al., 1998; Pang, 1995). For more information, please refer to the section on Parent Roles and Responsibilities in Chapter 3.

Parental Perception of the Teacher's and School's Roles and Responsibilities

Within the Confucian society, parents respect teachers and the school as an institution. Teachers are revered as authority figures, following heaven, earth, the emperor, and parents. The Chinese saying, "He who was once your teacher is your father for the rest of your life," reminds people to always obey and respect teachers. Perceived as a moral role model and a repository of knowledge, the teacher is expected to instill values, impart knowledge, transmit skills, and guide students toward the right path (Chung, 1997; Ho, 1994; Huntsinger, Jose, & Larson, 1998; Siu, 1992a; Yao, 1985). Parent-teacher relationships are built upon mutual respect and trust. When parents send their children to school, they expect teachers and the school to fulfill their roles and responsibilities as "dispensers of knowledge" and "molders of character" (Siu, 1992; Yao, 1985). "Teaching without strictness is the negligence of the teacher," as stated in a 13th-century classic, defines the long-established and still-maintained expectation of strict discipline.

Teachers are perceived as professionals, and parents often believe that they are not in any position to interfere with the teacher's teaching and the operation of the school. A teacher's and/or school's failure to meet the parents' expectation often results in distrust in the teacher and dissatisfaction with the school. According to Ho (1994) and Siu (1996a), the most frequent complaints about American schools by Chinese American parents are lax discipline, lack of moral education, poor math training, and insufficient homework.

Education System in the Homelands

Public education became available to the children in the cities of China shortly after the demise of the last dynasty and the founding of the Republic in 1912. Civil strife among the warlords, followed by the Japanese invasion and the battle for power between the communists and the nationalists, diverted national attention and resources for nearly 50 years and impeded the expansion of public education. It was not until the civil war between the communists and the nationalists ended in 1949 that a big push to educate the masses in both Mainland China and Taiwan became a reality.

The Western-style (American) public education system was the model when public education first was envisioned. Children in China, Hong Kong, and Taiwan all start school (1st grade) at age 6. Kindergarten is not part of the public school system yet, although preschool (also called kindergarten) attendance is very high, especially in Hong Kong, in Taiwan, and in bigger cities in China. The 6-3-3-4 system (i.e., six years of elementary school, three years each for junior and senior high schools, and four years of college for a baccalaureate degree) has been in place for more than 80 years. In 1986, China expanded the compulsory education portion to nine years. Within 15 years, 85 percent of the areas in China have made the extended compulsory education available (Gu, 2001).

Entrance to senior high school and universities involves keen competition. Only an extremely small percentage of the brightest students gain admission to higher education. Taiwan follows the same 6-3-3-4 system, but started the nine-year compulsory education system earlier (in 1968). Opportunities for higher education in

Taiwan are more plentiful due to the availability of many colleges and universities, but the competition for top institutions is also extremely tough as many students seek entrance. The annual college entrance examination, which involves tens of thousands of students, is considered a national event. For students who cannot make it to the academic track, options of technical schools and junior colleges in China, Taiwan, and Hong Kong are available. Hong Kong has had a different education system, with a strong British influence.

Each government encourages the establishment of proprietary and nonprofit private schools at all levels, although it was a new trend, reestablished in the Mainland, in the last two decades. Some of the long-established private schools are missionary schools, or they are affiliated with Christian churches, especially in Hong Kong. A very few schools have been established fairly recently by Buddhist groups in Taiwan. Most private schools are independently established by private groups with no religious affiliation.

Parents of public school students do not pay tuition, but they do pay some fees for activities, books, and supplies. The elementary level is the least expensive. The fees increase at the junior high level, even though it is within the compulsory education program. Parents of students in public senior high schools and colleges pay tuition in addition to fees. Compared to private schools, public schools and universities usually are considered a bargain in terms of quality and expense.

Similarities and Differences Between Chinese and American Schools

Schools in China, Taiwan, or Hong Kong are usually large, with high teacher-student ratios. Due to high population density, it is not unusual to see an elementary school crammed with thousands of students in a comparatively small space. Classroom buildings usually are several stories high, especially in urban areas. The teacher-pupil ratio in elementary schools is around 1:40, but slightly lower in Taiwan, Hong Kong, and Shanghai. The ratio is higher in secondary schools. Most lower elementary grades are self-contained, with a homeroom teacher who teaches most of the subjects, although teachers who specialize in a single subject (such as physical education, music, arts and craft, or English) also teach classes. In the upper elementary grades, each class is assigned a homeroom teacher, who is responsible for the class and who usually teaches one of the main subjects, such as Chinese reading and language arts, math, or science. Several other teachers instruct in other specialized subjects. In other words, it is more departmentalized in the higher grades, and students have more teachers. The homeroom teacher usually stays with the class for two years. In contrast with the practice in the United States, where the class is known by the teacher's last name, each Chinese class has a name of it own. The name may be as simple as Three-One, which indicates grade three, class one. More often, classes are named after a virtue or an aspiration, such as Three Righteousness or Three Loyalty.

As in the United States, most elementary teachers in Chinese schools are female. Although no statistics are available for comparison, the number of male elementary teachers appears to be higher in China than it is in the United States. Male teachers are more visible in junior high and even more so in senior high schools. In Chinese school and society, "Teacher" is a title like "Professor." Students and parents address the teacher by calling her or him "Teacher," or

"Teacher" followed by her or his family name. For example, Teacher Lin is a title for Mr. Lin or Miss Lin or a married female teacher whose maiden name is Lin. College students also call a professor "Teacher" followed by his or her surname, although in public the professor generally is addressed as "Professor" followed by his or her family name. Since the Chinese operate from a more formal framework, teachers and other staff at school also address fellow teachers formally. "Principal," like "Teacher," is also a title. Students, teachers, and other school staff call the head of the school "Principal," often followed by his or her surname. The principal, teachers, and other school staff call a student by his or her full name, although more and more teachers have begun to call students by their given names.

In Taiwan, almost all elementary schools are co-educational and students wear uniforms to school; the dress code has been relaxed considerably, however, and pupils are allowed to dress casually at least one or two days a week to encourage their self-expression and creativity. Secondary schools are either co-ed or single-gender schools. Nearly all secondary students wear uniforms; the uniforms have been updated and student involvement in the selection and design of the uniforms is encouraged. The extremely rigid regulations on hairstyle also have given way to a more progressive and open attitude. Schools that are considered prestigious, whether public or private, follow a long tradition of being gender-segregated.

In Mainland China and Taiwan, elementary schools are in session for six to seven hours, while secondary

schools are in session for seven to eight hours. Students in Hong Kong face overcrowded conditions. Therefore, their school days are shorter because of the need to squeeze two sessions in a day. In Taiwan, 1st- and 2nd-graders attend school only for half a day. In China and Taiwan, schools hold classes five days a week; schools in Hong Kong also are in session every other Saturday for half a day. In Mainland China and Taiwan, the school year begins in September; students are on break for three to four weeks, starting around late January or

early February, depending on the timing of the Chinese New Year. The school year ends at the end of June and students take a two-month summer vacation. In Hong Kong, students have two weeks off for Christmas and Chinese New Year and a one-week holiday for Easter, in addition to the long summer vacation.

School is considered a place where children learn discipline and adherence to orderliness, spurred on by the traditional belief that students must learn to take care of their own learning environment. Therefore, keeping the entire school clean and tidy is an integral part of schooling and the responsibility of the student body. Elementary and secondary students in China and Taiwan are involved in cleaning the whole school, inside and out, including offices, classrooms, restrooms, and the schoolyard. A morning clean-up time takes place before classes, and another one follows at the end of the day. Students dust desks, shine windows, sweep floors, rake leaves, scrub the toilets, and do other cleaning chores. Often, these cleaning chores are ones they don't do, are not willing to do, or are excused from doing at home. A school of several thousand students may have only two or three custodians. Most of the housekeeping chores are taken care of by the students and are considered an integral part of the "life education."

Except for preschools (called kindergartens) and a few exclusive private schools, schools do not provide buses to transport students. Students walk, take the public bus, or are driven to school. While hot lunches are provided for free or for a fee at some schools, depending on the family income, most students bring their own boxed lunch from home and pay a small fee to have it heated (steamed, usually) at the school.

Differences in Classroom Interactions

Classroom interactions in Chinese schools are more formal than in America. The student attitude toward the teacher has always been one of great respect. In Hong Kong and Taiwan, such interactions have become less formal in recent years, and thus not as formal as in China. Nonetheless, certain decorums are still expected. In Taiwan, for example, students rise to greet and bow to the teacher before class and repeat the procedure, after the class, to thank the teacher. Students are expected to raise their hands and wait for a turn to speak until called upon by the teacher. Students are not allowed to leave the classroom without permission from the teacher. A bathroom break is to be taken during recess, which lasts only 10 to 15 minutes and happens every 40 to 50 minutes. The longest recess is the lunch break, which may last for 45 minutes to over an hour.

The teacher usually speaks to the whole class, standing in front by the chalkboard. S/he may also circulate from row to row of desks to offer assistance or monitor independent study. Some teachers arrange the classrooms differently by grouping desks and chairs into pods to facilitate group projects and encourage cooperative learning. Besides a class leader (who often is selected by the teacher in the lower grades and elected by classmates in higher grades), other student officers are selected or elected to take charge of various roles and responsibilities, such as monitoring the housekeeping of the classroom or the conduct of peers.

The classroom interactions sometimes appear to be authoritarian; as was discussed in Chapter 3, however, cultural factors need to be taken into consideration, and therefore the authoritative style most likely is a better description. For the most part, interactions between the teacher and the students are initiated by the teacher. Students are passive recipients, not active constructors or seekers of knowledge. The teaching-learning dynamic is characterized by the mimetic approach (Gardner, 1989). The teacher is perceived as the repository of knowledge, and the students as vessels to be filled. Thus, the teacher takes an expository approach by presenting mini lectures, giving directions, and assigning tasks while the students listen, observe, take notes, imitate, and follow instructions.

Stevenson et al. (1986) reported that Chinese students were led more by the teachers than their American counterparts were. Chinese teachers spent proportionally more time imparting information than American teachers did. Procedural and/or clarification questions are the most common question types. Students generally do not ask questions challenging the teacher's point of view; in recent years, however, students have been encouraged to become critical thinkers. The teacher demonstrates or explains what and how to do something, and the students learn through repetition. The basic classroom decorum requires quiet, attentive, and orderly behavior. Raising one's hand too often, volunteering answers too often, or asking too many questions may be considered showing off (Cheng, 1999).

Although a few more progressive teachers and urban schools are slowly moving away from the traditional practices, most teaching and learning is content-based instead of student-centered. Acquisition of factual knowledge is strongly emphasized, and instruction is direct and explicit. Textbooks essentially drive the teaching and learning processes, with limited teacher creativity and few student-initiated explorations. Grades are based primarily on tests that require

recall of factual information (Cheng, 1998). Due to large class size and high teacher-student ratios, individualized attention is very limited. Most of the activities are either whole-class activities or individual assignments. Occasionally, the teacher may assign group activities.

Because most students are relatively well-behaved in class, compared to students in American schools, the teacher usually does not have too many classroom management problems. The teacher generally deals with minor misbehaviors in the classroom and sends perpetrators of major transgressions to one of the deans (similar to a vice principal) who is in charge of handling discipline problems, among other duties.

As Cheng (1998, 1999) pointed out, different expectations concerning classroom discourse in American and Chinese schools may result in ambivalence and confusion. American schools encourage creativity, exploration, student initiation and discovery, assertiveness, and risk-taking. American teachers expect students to be interactive and participatory as well as to engage in critical thinking and problem solving. Some more progressive Chinese teachers and well-educated parents also encourage similar classroom interactions. The majority of Chinese parents and teachers, however, expect students to be quiet, obedient, and attentive, and not to challenge or question the teacher. Such conflicting expectations, along with different communication and interaction styles, often cause confusion among Chinese American students and misinterpretation and frustration for American teachers. The Chinese classroom interaction style is influenced by culturally related expectations, and so is characterized by risk avoidance and lack of assertiveness; delay, hesitation, and passivity in response and discourse participation; speaking softly and giving short responses; and showing great concern for grades and examination results. The following communication styles typically found among Chinese can be confusing for American teachers: frowning to show concentration (rather than displeasure), avoidance of eye and physical contact, blushing or showing embarrassment over praise, and smiling enigmatically (Cheng, 1999; Trueba et al., 1993).

Learning Styles of Chinese Students

In spite of the dangers inherent in overgeneralizing about a specific culture, it has been suggested that Chinese cultural values of perseverance, restraint, and patience may account for the culture's learning style, which transfers particularly well to spatial and numerical reasoning and not as well to verbal learning (Gardner, 1980). Chinese children have been found to score higher on spatial, numerical, or nonverbal intelligence tests, and less well on tests of verbal ability (Huntsinger, Larson, Krieg, & Balsink, 1998; Kitano, 1980). The SAT verbal and math scores are excellent examples to illustrate this disparity. According to data from the College Board (Fong, 2002), the average verbal and math sub-scores of Asian Americans differed by more than 60 points on tests taken between 1997 and 1999, by far the largest difference in scores among any of the ethnic groups represented. Hispanic and White students scored practically the same on both parts of the test, while African Americans' scores showed a 10-point margin. Ho (1994) suggests that Chinese people's restraint on verbal assertiveness and the mimetic approach of the teaching-learning dynamics, which he termed cognitive conservatism, might relate to the differences in Chinese students' relative weakness in verbal abili-

ties and in divergent thinking.

It has been suggested that Asian students tend to be field-dependent or structure-oriented learners (Zhang & Carrasquillo, 1995). They learn best in well-structured, quiet environments. Since the Chinese equate the printed page with learning and Chinese writing depends on a code that visually labels ideas instead of sounds (as in English), Chinese students are therefore more visually oriented and seem to need the reinforcement of reading and writing exercises (Wu, 1982; Young & Lum, 1982). Asian children are more dependent on their teacher for guidance and are inclined to seek the teacher's approval for decisions they make (Wu, 1982; Yao, 1985). The Chinese student tends to have a highly reflective response style that requires additional "wait-time" in order to respond to questions (Kitano, 1980; Pikcunas, 1986). Asian students are less likely to reveal or volunteer their opinions, tend to avoid showing off their abilities, and rarely challenge instructors. They seek conformity, obedience, and group dependence. Since their culture expects them to be passive learners in the classroom, Chinese students often wait for the teacher to deliver the lesson, even if the lesson has been delivered through class discussion and participation (New York City Board of Education, 1989).

Conversely and interestingly, the learning approach favored and emphasized in the culture seems to compensate for Chinese people's weakness in verbal abilities. Ho (1994) suggests that the learning styles of recitation, rote memorization, and drill and repetition are related to the sacred quality of the written words in Confucianism. He contends that students' preoccupation with examinations, and their syllabus-bound approach to study, are in accordance with the Confucian emphasis on mastering a body of knowledge. Following the tradition, preschool children in Taiwan and China are taught to recite classical verses without fully understanding the meaning (Lin, 2002; Miller et al., 1997; Zhang, 2001). They appear to enjoy the recitation, presumably due to the enjoyment associated with the rhythm and rhymes. Elementary and secondary students in Taiwan are required to memorize most of the Chinese reading and language texts, especially the well-known classics. Secondary and tertiary students in Taiwan and Hong Kong rely heavily on rote memorization to prepare for examinations.

Because of their preoccupation with grades and entrance examinations, many students are willing to memorize or drill the sequential steps or procedures to solve an advanced math problem, even if they do not understand the problem. Ho (1994) reports that tertiary students in Hong Kong are so examination-oriented that they often concentrate their efforts only on materials covered in the class, rely on handouts and notes, and use only those texts and/or recommended readings that will prepare them for examinations. Secondary and college students in Taiwan are similar to their counterparts in Hong Kong—they are admirably and diligently studious, but with a very narrow focus. They spend an inordinate amount of time reading, doing homework, memorizing, drilling, and repeating, but not manipulating, exploring, discovering, researching, analyzing, inferring, thinking critically, or solving complex, real-life problems.

Linguistic Issues

As discussed earlier, the Chinese language is non-alphabetic, monosyllabic, tonal, and non-inflectional. The lack of inflection and derivation appears to pose the most trouble for Chinese-speaking students who are learning English as a second language. In addition, differences between the phonological, syntactic, and lexical structures of Chinese and English may result in some difficulties in listening, speaking, reading, and writing English (Buckley, 1997; Cheng, 1991; Chi, 1999; Tinloy et al., 1988).

In terms of pronunciation, some English phonemes do not exist in Chinese; others are similar but not identical, causing confusion. Some challenging consonant and vowel sounds, consonant clusters, and endings, along with polysyllables, stress, and intonation, often create difficulties for some Chinese speakers. Challenging consonants or consonant clusters include: *l, r, wh, th, ch, sh, dg, z,* as well as such three-letter clusters as *spl, spr, shr.* Difficult ending sounds for Chinese include most English words with a voiced consonant ending and allomorphs in the plural and past tense morphemes. Compared to vowels, consonants are, in fact, easier for some Chinese to pronounce. It is harder for some Chinese speakers to hear the contrast between long and short vowels and pronounce them accurately. Vowel digraphs, diphthongs, and the r-controlled vowels are quite challenging for Chinese speakers. The stress or accent to emphasize a particular syllable in a polysyllabic word also poses challenges for Chinese students. It is not an easy task for some Chinese students to break up a word's syllables, accent the appropriate stressed syllable, put the syllables together, and then pronounce the word correctly. Finally, Chinese tones affect individual words rather than sentences. Chinese students may have difficulty with English sentence intonation patterns (Buckley, 1997; Cheng, 1991; Chi, 1999; Tinloy et al., 1988).

The most common grammatical errors that Chinese students make usually are associated with the differences in morphology and syntax between the Chinese and English languages.

Such features of English grammar as articles, plurals, classifiers, subject-verb agreement, and verb tense often cause great difficulty for Chinese students (Chi, 1999). Older Chinese immigrants who have achieved a high level of proficiency in English often find they still face problems with these concepts.

Besides the challenges in pronunciation and grammar, the two languages also present differences in vocabulary and in oral and written discourse. It is not unusual to see Chinese-speaking students exhibiting the influences or characteristics of the Chinese language in vocabulary usage and/or in oral and written discourse when speaking English. Understanding the differences between Chinese and English languages will help provide insight into the causes of the difficulties Chinese students face when learning English (Chi, 1999; Tinloy et al., 1988). A detailed discussion of that topic is beyond the scope of this book, however.

Academic Success and Difficulty

Polarized Academic Performances

Asian Americans constitute only 4 percent of the U.S. population and Asian Americans make up even a smaller percentage of the American student population, yet their academic success has drawn much attention and discussion in the last two decades. From kindergarten to graduate school, Asian Americans' grades, test scores, admission rates to top universities, and success at winning competitions have captured extensive media coverage, fascinated many people, and fueled research aimed at identifying the underlying factors. Since the 1980s, Asian American students have made a strong presence at the Intel (formerly Westinghouse) Science Talent Search, among the Presidential Scholars, and have shown disproportionately high representation in the student bodies of the most selective universities. For example, in 2002, six out of the 17 finalists of the Siemens Westinghouse Math, Science & Technology Competition were Chinese-Americans (Ning, 2002). In 2003, 29 of the 137 Presidential Scholars were Chinese Americans (Liu, 2003). Asian Americans make up 14 percent, 12 percent, and 24 percent of the undergraduate populations at Yale, Harvard, and Stanford, respectively (Fong, 2002). The Web site of University of California, Berkeley indicates that, in 2002, 39 percent of its students were Asian Americans. Among these overachievers, Chinese Americans lead the ethnic breakdown, constituting approximately one third to more than one half of the total honors awarded. These extraordinary academic achievements have drawn a subtle backlash. Perceiving Asian Americans as an "over-represented minority," the most prestigious colleges and universities in the United States allegedly imposed quotas to limit the admission of Asian American students. Although no university admitted any deliberate quotas against Asian Americans, several universities did acknowledge some flaws or even apologized for their admission policies.

While the whiz kids get the attention they certainly deserve, many Chinese American children can be found at the other extreme, suffering in obscurity from academic difficulty and failure. These students often drop out of school and join gangs, receiving no attention until they make headlines by committing a crime. In this section, both phenomena will be discussed, along with explanations of contributing factors.

Theories of Academic Success

The relatively recent phenomenon of Asian student success has fascinated many researchers, who have suggested and debated several theoretical explanations, including selective immigration, and genetic, cultural, sociological, and historical factors. The 1965 Immigration Act, which favored educated and skilled immigrants, is believed to have contributed to the remarkable academic achievement of Chinese American students, especially those from upper-middle class families originating from, or whose parents originated from, Taiwan and Hong Kong (and, in recent years, China) (Hirschman & Wong, 1986; Siu, 1992a).

Regardless of the extent to which selective immigration may have contributed to school success, Chinese newspapers published in the United States frequently report on the outstanding achievements of Chinese American students and other success stories of Chinese American individuals, most of whom were either born or have one or both parents born overseas in Hong Kong or Taiwan and, in recent years, China.

Related to selected immigration is the controversial belief in genetic factors. Some scholars theorize that Asian Americans' high level of academic achievement is a result of superior intelligence (Jensen, 1973; Rushton, 1985; Vernon, 1982). However, a highly acclaimed and rigorous study led by Stevenson and colleagues (Stevenson et al., 1985) found no evidence to support this belief. A less controversial and more commonly accepted explanation is cultural influences. Many scholars argue that traditional Confucian values have a strong influence on the parent-child dynamics, ultimately resulting in an exceptionally high level of school performance.

Another theoretical perspective is conceptualized around the interactions of sociological and historical factors. Recognizing the influences of cultural and family socialization, Sue and Okazaki (1990) contend that

because of limited opportunities in noneducational areas, educational achievement has become feasible, functional, and critical to Asians. In other words, education is perceived as a viable means for social and financial upward mobility, especially in light of difficulties in other areas associated with language barriers and social discrimination.

As Chen and Stevenson (1995) stated, logical arguments can be offered for each of these theories. However, that is not the focus of this book. Neither is there enough empirical data to validate their proposals at this point. Since this book is intended to provide educators and service providers with information to better understand Asian Americans, cultural factors supporting academic success will be discussed in detail, although this does not imply the author's sole support of this theoretical perspective. This information should not be taken to perpetuate teachers' stereotyped perceptions of Chinese American students and parents, nor should it be used to mislead Chinese American parents into believing in the superiority of these cultural factors.

Cultural Factors Related to Academic Performance

Parental Attitudes. The school success of Chinese American students has been correlated with Confucian beliefs, cultural attitudes, and parent/child interactions. More specifically, Chinese parents place a very high value on education, respect teachers and schools, shape positive attitudes toward learning, expect and demand high standards, believe in the role of effort in academic achievement, structure and monitor their children's free time and social activities, eliminate distractions that may interfere with their children's studies, excuse the child from making economic contributions and doing household chores, invest in educational activities and programs, and create a home environment conducive to learning (Asakawa & Csikszentmihalyi, 1998; Chao, 1996b; Caplan, Choy, & Whitmore, 1992; Chen & Stevenson, 1995; Chiang, 2000; Fejgin, 1995; Fong, 2002; Huntsinger, Jose, & Ching, 1994; Huntsinger, Jose, & Larson, 1998; Huntsinger, Larson, Krieg, & Balsink, 1998; Huntsinger, Schoeneman, & Ching, 1994; Lee & Rong, 1988; Mau, 1997; Mordkowitz & Ginsburg, 1986; Schickedanz, 1995; Schneider & Lee, 1990; Siu, 1992a, 1992b, 1994; Trueba et al., 1993; Uba, 1994; Wong, 1995; Yee et al., 1998; Young, 1998; Zhang & Carrasquillo, 1995). Chinese students also take education seriously. East Asian students' academic success has been linked to the values and aspirations they share with their parents. Chinese American parents, as discussed in detail in Chapter 3, expend great effort to facilitate their children's academic success by valuing education, expecting high standards and aspirations, respecting teachers and schools, and steering children's focus on education. Chinese students' beliefs, attitudes, and practices in terms of academic focus will be discussed below.

Student Attitudes. The Confucian influence on students' attitudes, beliefs, and practices in education has been deeply rooted and far-reaching. Many Chinese students willingly work to meet their parents and teachers' expectations for academic excellence (Chang, 1973). Studies show that Asian American students are more interested in school (Wong, 1995) and have more positive attitudes toward education (Fejgin, 1995). In a study comparing Chinese American and European American high school students, Chinese American students were found to aspire to attend more selective colleges and universities,

participate more in the arts and in academic extracurricular activities, spend more time doing homework, and engage less in social activities or jobs (Huntsinger et al., 1997). Chinese elementary students also thought more about schoolwork on their way to school, engaged more in academic activities, and were more likely to mention education-related goals than American children were (Chen, 1989). Furthermore, Asian students were significantly happier, enjoyed themselves more, and felt better about themselves when engaged in more serious, work-like activities (Asakawa & Csikszentmihalyi, 1998).

Effort. Moreover, Chinese students share their parents' belief that effort, rather than innate ability, determines academic achievement (Chao, 1996b; Chen & Stevenson, 1995; Fong, 2002; Ho, 1994; Leung, 1991; Leung, Maehr, & Harnisch, 1993; Schickedanz, 1995; Siu, 1992a, 1992b; Zhang & Carrasquillo, 1995). Reminded by parents and teachers of the proverbs "practice makes perfect" and "diligence can make up for deficiencies," Chinese American students spend more time on homework and less time watching television, playing video games, partying with friends, or dating (Huntsinger et al., 1997; Mau, 1997; Schickedanz, 1995). Chinese American students take more challenging courses, and are less likely to miss school, cut class, or be late to school than other Asian students or than white or black students. Chinese American students are more likely to take tutorial or supplementary sessions to enhance their achievement, or to enroll in language, art, and music lessons outside of school. They often take part in educational and cultural activities, such as visiting museums and libraries. They have higher educational expectations and aspirations and are more likely to aspire to professional careers than white students

(Huntsinger, Jose, & Larson, 1998; Peng & Wright, 1994; Trueba et al., 1993; Wong, 1995). With parental and teacher support, achieving Chinese students start planning for college and preparing for the SAT/ACT exams early, and they focus on forging a bright future via higher education.

Academic Difficulties

While it appears that Chinese American students are exceptional students, many do struggle in the classroom or drop out of school. Problems may stem from limited English proficiency, and are compounded by the lack of bilingual support from the school and the parents' inability to help. Immigrant students' success in making the transition to an English-speaking classroom often depends on their age when they first immigrate, their primary language skills, and their English proficiency. Generally speaking, the younger the student, the easier it is to make the transition. A solid foundation in primary language literacy, and an academic background, also help with the transition, as does a high level of English proficiency. Well-to-do families headed by educated parents usually have more resources to help an immigrant student. In communities with a large population of Chinese Americans, tutorial services are easily available—at least for those families who can afford them. Unfortunately, children whose parents speak little or no English, are from lower socioeconomic backgrounds, or live in smaller towns or inner cities without bilingual support from school often are lost and left alone to sink or swim. Some older Chinese immigrant students from rural areas of the Fujian and Guangdong provinces often find it hard to survive an American middle or high school with their limited

English skills. Another problem is the insufficient number of bilingual teachers or bilingual instructional assistants. Without bilingual support, both Chinese immigrant parents and students of lower socioeconomic background find navigating schools in America intimidating and frustrating.

Chinese American Students at Risk

Poverty and Distractions From Academic Focus. Related to academic difficulty are issues that place some Chinese American students at risk socially and academically. Chinese Americans are said to be the most polarized among Asian Americans in terms of socioeconomic status (Min, 1995, cited in Siu, 1996b). As a result, the education performances of the children of the two extremes vary greatly. The needs and risk factors of the children from lower socioeconomic backgrounds are very acute. While many Chinese American children are excused from household chores, shielded from other academic distractions and interferences, encouraged to devote all their attention to studying, and receive tutorial help, some less fortunate Chinese American students are expected to contribute to the family earnings by taking after-school jobs that leave them exhausted, unable to concentrate on schoolwork, and without adequate time to study (Huang, 2002; Siu, 1996b). One study reported that some parents in New York's Chinatown, pressed by economic necessity, reportedly urged children who were not doing well academically to quit school and get full-time jobs (Sim, 1992).

Lack of Parental Support and Supervision. Some newer immigrants with limited education or resources have no choice but to work long hours in low-paying jobs, sometimes far away from their families. Their pervasive absence from the family, due to the long working hours or faraway job sites, poses social problems for spouses, parents, and children. Children who came as unaccompanied minors or were left alone in the United States to attend school (the so-called parachute students or little foreign students) have to fend for themselves. With no parental support or supervision, they have to cope with emotional, academic, and other problems on their own. They often end up staying out late, loitering in the streets to seek support from peers, and falling under the influences of negative peer pressure. Even parents who are present at home regularly may not be able to help their children with schoolwork. Their own limited education level and English proficiency prevent them from helping their children (Siu, 1996b).

Risk Factors in School and Societal Contexts. Besides the aforementioned familial risk factors, Siu (1996b) also identifies other risk factors in school and societal contexts, including inadequate assessment, placement, and evaluation; inappropriate grade retention policies and practices associated with English proficiency; poor quality and/or availability of instruction by a trained and/or bilingual staff; inadequate orientation and parental involvement programs; a hostile racial and social climate; and a lack of cultural affirmation. The issue of a school's racial and social climate deserves special attention. Siu (1996b) reported that some students from lower socioeconomic backgrounds were treated insensitively by school personnel and encountered hostility and prejudice. Risk in the community and societal contexts includes the stereotype of the model minority, inadequate community support programs, and the interaction of multiple risk factors. The

model minority stereotype is particularly troubling, as it masks the needs of those who are in desperate need of support. The interactive and cumulative effect of these multiple factors is overwhelming, setting up the poor, non- or limited English-speaking Chinese immigrant students for failure.

Parental Pressure and Academic Stress

The high educational achievements of Chinese American students are not attained without some negative side effects. Although many highly motivated, successful, and well-rounded students maintain their social and emotional well-being, some academically high-achieving students suffer various levels of parental pressure and related psychological stress. Chinese newspapers report on Chinese American high school or college students committing suicide, or attempting to commit suicide, due to academically related stress or failing to meet their parents' high academic expectations.

Thus, the high educational goals that Chinese parents value dearly often serve as a double-edged sword. They propel students to succeed and pressure them to do their very best. Believing in the axioms that "practice makes perfect" and "diligence can make up for deficiencies," some parents set unrealistically high goals, overlooking the limitations of their children. They pin their hopes on their children, perceiving them as extensions of their own dreams. Academic success is related to honor, pride, and happiness, while failure is viewed as reflecting their own shortcomings as parents. A child easily senses the pressure and feels guilt if he or she does not quite live up to these expectations.

The stress, anxiety, guilt, and shame are exacerbated if the parents have made considerable sacrifices and the student is not academically gifted. Some Chinese parents are overly concerned or obsessed with grades, test scores, class rank, honor rolls, and gaining admission to higher education institutions. Some parents not only expect but also demand extremely high levels of achievement. When they see a "B" on a report card, they are often as overtly alarmed as if they saw an "F." This kind of inordinate expectation, demand, and overreaction to less than perfect academic performance subjects their children to undue test anxiety and tremendous stress. Failure to meet expectations is perceived as the result of a lack of effort, thus inducing guilt and admonishment. Moreover, parents make matters worse by comparing their children's academic performances with siblings' academic achievements, or with those of the children of their relatives or acquaintances. Chinese American students, no matter their academic standing, resent this practice tremendously. Practices like these often lead to parent-child conflicts; the students feel self-doubt and alienation, are depressed, and display other problems (Chung, 1997; Fong, 2002; Huang, 1993; Lorenzo, Frost, & Reinherz, 2000; Shen & Mo, 1990; Uba, 1994; Wong, 1995).

The academic stress Chinese American students experience seems to relate to or be compounded by parental pressure to succeed, as opposed to the academic stress most students experience from time to time. In studies comparing high-achieving students, Chinese students reported the least stress, while their American counterparts reported the most stress (Crystal et al., 1994; Fuligni & Stevenson, 1995).

Due to the paucity of research and literature available on the topic, not much is known about other psychological issues regarding Chinese American students. Although limited information suggests that

Chinese American students may have a lower physical self-image than black or white American students, or rate themselves lower on competency and acceptance than European Americans, this might have to do more with the self-effacement tendency of the Chinese people (Huntsinger et al., 1997; Stigler, Smith, & Mao, 1985). Humility is a highly valued Chinese virtue; being overly assertive is considered distasteful. Most Chinese people shy away from being boastful. It is very likely that Chinese American students were on the conservative side when rating themselves.

Parental Involvement and Interactions With Teachers and the School

Chinese American parents' involvement in their children's education varies greatly. According to Siu (1996a), the factors affecting the patterns of Chinese American parents' involvement include how long they have lived in the United States, acculturation, familiarity with the American education system, perception of their status in the United States, English language proficiency, work schedules, perceptions of parental and the school's roles and responsibilities, and their school's efforts to involve families. Siu further analyzed the types of Chinese American parents and their perceptions of parental involvement. U.S.-born and -schooled parents who are secure with their status in the United States view themselves as partners with the school. They are more likely to be active and visible at the school, serving as volunteers or policymakers and contributing their skills, talents, and time. Immigrant parents who were schooled overseas and do not feel economically secure often hold a different point of view regarding parental involvement. They regard teachers as professionals, consequently leaving decisions to the school and teachers. They quietly supplement and support their children's learning behind the scenes, at home. Parents born and schooled overseas but who also attended school in the United States tend to fall in between these two parts of the spectrum.

Although English-speaking Chinese parents tend to become more assertive when they become acculturated, newly immigrated parents are often quiet, polite, submissive, and cooperative. Furthermore, they hold a different view regarding the roles and responsibilities of parents and teachers. They have a great deal of respect for, and confidence in, teachers. They tend to leave their children's schooling to the educational professionals and believe that parents should not interfere with school policies (Huang, 1993; Shen & Mo, 1990; Siu, 1996a; Yao, 1988). Some might even view communication with teachers as "checking up" on teachers or challenging their authority, which is considered disrespectful. Some become perplexed at the need for parental involvement in the classroom or regard teachers who seek parental involvement as incompetent or non-professional.

Newly arrived parents usually do not initiate contact with teachers. When contacted by the teacher or school, they often are quiet and attentive listeners, willing to cooperate but asking few questions or volunteering little information (Yao, 1988). Some teachers become frustrated with Chinese American parents who ignore school notices, viewing them as nonresponsive or uncaring about their children. As Siu (1996a) explains, Chinese-American parents, like parents of any other ethnic group, vary in the amount of time, money, and energy they can invest in their children's education. Newer immigrants, especially those who are at the lower end of the socioeconomic level, may

have to work long and odd hours and thus are not available during the daytime to meet with teachers. They may not speak English or understand the note sent home. They may not have transportation to get to the school. Some newer immigrant mothers might not have learned to drive yet. Some may not feel comfortable in the school environment.

Although some Chinese immigrant parents may not appear to be that interested and involved in their children's education, especially at the school site, they often are very involved, both directly and indirectly, with their children at home. Some parents directly tutor or teach their children, help with or check over their children's homework, devise and assign extra homework, and closely supervise after-school time and other free time. Some parents offer indirect types of support, such as hiring a tutor, enrolling their children in supplementary programs (including music, arts, and language classes), purchasing extra workbooks, and excusing their children from household chores (Chao, 1996a, 1996b; Chiang, 2000; Huntsinger, Jose, & Larson, 1998; Huntsinger, Larson, Krieg, & Balsink, 1998; Siu, 1996a).

Heritage Language School

As stated in Chapter 3, preserving and passing down the cultural heritage to their children is near and dear to the hearts of Chinese American parents. Many parents encourage, push, coerce, or force their children to attend Chinese school. Although it is called a Chinese school, it is primarily a Chinese language class. A few small Chinese school facilities also serve other functions for the Chinese communities in bigger metropolitan areas. Classes usually meet on a public school campus, in a church, or in a community center on weekends for two to three hours at a time, or for half a day. Some programs may be more intensive, holding classes three or more days a week after school or in the early evenings. Literacy in Chinese reading and writing is the main mission of heritage language schools. In addition, summer language and culture camps are gaining popularity. Mandarin is the medium for instruction, although a smaller number of schools use Cantonese, due to their desire to maintain a close relationship with Cantonese-speaking relatives, especially grandparents who do not speak Mandarin. Parents' limited proficiency in Mandarin and concern over lack of reinforcement and usage at home are the other considerations for continuing to use Cantonese as the medium of instruction. Students are placed according to language competency, age, and family background. There are two types of classes. One is for native speakers and the other is for English speakers and speakers of another dialect. Chinese history and cultural activities, such as Chinese folk dance, martial arts, Chinese songs, calligraphy, brush painting, Chinese chess, along with computer courses in Chinese and ball games, are incorporated to balance out the language and literacy lessons, which require a lot of practice, repetition, and memorization.

Going to Chinese school after "regular" school, in the evenings or on weekends, is not something that most Chinese American youngsters enjoy. It is a weekly struggle for children and parents in many households. Most parents simply give up the battle by the time their children reach upper elementary or junior high age. However, interest in Chi-

nese language school is on the rise because of increasing recognition and confirmation of the Chinese language by formal educational institutions and on standardized tests, such as the SAT II Chinese Language Test. Chinese heritage language schools across the United States have experienced an increase in the number of secondary school students continuing their attendance or reenrolling. Some students are motivated to earn high school credits. Some continue the class for preparation for the SAT II Chinese Language Test. Some come to do community service, serving as teacher assistants. And some come for social reasons, meeting and socializing with childhood friends who do not go to the same schools as they do. Nonetheless, some come with genuine interest and an

intrinsic desire to learn more about their culture and heritage. In fact, the number of students of Chinese descent who attended Chinese language schools and then take Chinese at the college level has increased (Wang, 1996). Also, more non-Chinese students, biracial (Chinese and other race) children, and Chinese girls adopted from Chinese orphanages by American families have been enrolling in Chinese language schools.

In contrast to private music lessons, which often are unaffordable to families with limited resources, nearly all Chinese schools are nonprofit, established and run by parents, and available to all the children in the Chinese community. Although a few for-profit programs are run in conjunction with private schools, child care centers, and tutorial programs in metropolitan areas, Chinese American children of all income levels have equal access to Chinese language schools in the community. (In smaller communities or communities with a smaller Chinese population, however, parents often have to drive quite a distance to the nearest Chinese language school.)

Parents elect the board of directors, the principal, and administrative officials, and they serve as teachers and volunteers at the schools. A small fee is charged for supplies, classroom rental, and insurance. Scholarships are available for those who cannot afford to pay. Teachers are paid a small stipend for their service. Most schools use teaching materials developed and provided by the government in Taiwan, which also provides staff development and newsletters offering lessons and teaching ideas. Recently, a small but increasing number of schools have adopted teaching materials developed in mainland China. Children whose parents are from China usually attend schools that teach Pinyin and a simplified form of script,

while the other children learn the traditional form of characters. There are more than 800 Chinese schools in the United States, ranging in size from a few dozen students to nearly 3,000 students (Yang, 2002).

Parental Perceptions of Extracurricular Activities

When it comes to education and schooling, academic areas are given a higher priority than other school activities. Academic achievement is heavily emphasized. While parents encourage their children to participate in extracurricular activities, the children are expected not to allow those activities to interfere with academic achievement. If academic performance drops, parents are quick to pull a child out of extracurricular activities and steer him or her back toward academics. Music appears to be the preferred extracurricular activity. Taking private piano or violin lessons is like a rite of passage for Chinese American children. Although elementary school children participate in soccer, swimming, and other sports, sports take a back seat by the time Chinese American children reach high school. There are several reasons why parents emphasize classical music instead of sports. A detailed discussion of this is presented in the Education and Schooling section of Chapter 3.

Implications and Recommendations

Administration and Leadership

Since school administrators and other education leaders are considered heads of schools and leaders of teachers, tremendous respect and enormous prestige are bestowed upon them. Thus, principals and other administrators are at an advantage from the beginning in providing education leadership to children and families of Chinese descent.

But that respect and prestige may only mean that parents willingly, respectfully, and quietly follow along and passively participate. Achieving the mainstream practices of higher levels of parental involvement, full collaboration, and mutual partnerships will prove to be learning tasks for parents and coaching tasks for administrators.

Understandably, there are no shortcuts or simple strategies to achieve the complex responsibility of providing culturally appropriate best practices in education to Chinese American children and families. Nevertheless, cultural literacy and staff development, community outreach and involvement, a bilingual/bicultural support system, and parent leadership empowerment practices are key areas where administrators can start.

Cultural Literacy and Staff Development.

The importance of knowing the Chinese perspectives described in this book cannot be overstated. Knowing the geographic origins, immigration reasons, language origins and linguistic issues, belief systems and values, communication styles, naming systems, and other relevant cultural information gives an administrator and school personnel a head start in cultural sensitivity. An awareness of the Chinese American family structure and dynamics, perception of children, parental roles and responsibilities, child's roles and responsibilities, parenting attitudes and practices, and child discipline gives an administrator and staff a peek into students' family lives. An understanding of these and other issues already brought to light in this book will provide insights in program planning and implementation. Having basic knowledge about the Chinese perspective regarding health, mental health, and health care, as well as about disabilities and intervention, is crucial in providing leadership in special education.

Parents are quick to discern the knowledge base and insights of administrators on things related to the Chinese. Administrators who shed light on insights regarding culture-specific information often win great admiration and respect. On the other hand, ignorance on administrators' part about the Chinese may prove costly; their credibility as education leaders is reduced and their effectiveness is weakened.

Education leadership also entails staff development to address the learning styles of Chinese American students and other pertinent education issues. As recommended by a New York City Board of Education Task Force (1989), all school staff need to receive sensitivity training regarding Asian American children. Teachers and counselors need training on methodology and material adaptation. Office staff need training on culturally sensitive interpersonal skills. Educators with expertise in this area, as well as parents and community leaders, would be good resources to turn to for insights. Administrators also have the responsibility of overseeing the incorporation, infusion, and integration of Chinese culture into curriculum and instruction. Examples of curriculum integration and lesson planning include: counting in Chinese; offering greetings and simple phrases and pleasantries in Chinese; singing Chinese songs and playing Chinese music; incorporating Chinese crafts and sports; comparing the Chinese version of Cinderella with other versions; comparing Chinese proverbs and their equivalents in other cultures; and researching the influences and contributions of Chinese Americans from historical and contemporary perspectives.

Community Outreach and Involvement.

Basic cultural literacy is only a start; ideally, the goal is cultural proficiency. One of the ways to progress toward higher levels of cultural literacy is reaching out to the community and participating in social and cultural activities and events. Visiting homes and businesses and participating in cultural events, such as Chinese New Year celebrations, are opportunities to immerse oneself in the sights, sounds, aromas, tastes, and ambience of the Chinese. Experiences like these open windows for education leaders to see the other side of their students' lives and see how families live and interact with each other. What is not seen at school, not heard or read about before, and generally not known to the administrators are, nonetheless, integral parts of their students' lives. These are the blind spots of educational leadership. In sum, firsthand experiences through direct involvement with the community often result in a better understanding of the Chinese perspective and spark ideas to better serve children of Chinese descent.

School administrators' visibility in the community has added benefits, beyond meeting parents and networking with community leaders. It sends a clear message to students, parents, and community leaders that the administrators respect the Chinese American community, value their culture, and are willing to reach out and network with them. It helps break down barriers and transcend the gaps between parents and school personnel. It provides opportunities for parents to see the other side of administrators, and helps parents feel more comfortable approaching and collaborating with school leaders. Many administrators and education leaders have recognized the importance of reaching out to the Chinese American community and have been actively involved in non-school-related events planned by the community. For example, administrators of several districts in the San Francisco Bay Area with high concentrations of Chinese American students have been attending the annual ceremony honoring the birthday of Confucius and celebrating Chinese Teachers' Day, held on a weekend in the early fall. Some districts have gone one step further by sending education leaders to Taiwan and Hong Kong to visit schools and take a firsthand look at their education systems and classroom interactions. Although direct links between administrators' involvement in the community and parental collaboration with school leaders have yet to be proven, partnerships have been getting more active. Several districts in the San Francisco Bay Area have had continuous representation from the Chinese American community on their school boards.

A Bilingual and Bicultural Support System. Regardless of the school leadership's cultural literacy level and community outreach efforts, a bilingual and bicultural support system needs to be established in order to link the school and the home, and to address the needs of the children and families. While different states have different policies and practices regarding bilingual education, the advantages of bilingual support to English language learners are clear. Bilingual education aside, building bilingual and bicultural support to bridge the school and home, facilitate communication and cross-cultural understanding, and foster cultural pride and bicultural and bilingual development is critical. Such a bilingual and bicultural support system includes program planning, support to English language learners, home-school connections, staffing, and staff development.

Since the ideal of having certified bilingual teachers is not always possible, a long-standing compromise is utilization of bilingual volunteers or paraprofessionals.

The volunteers and paraprofessionals assume the roles and responsibilities of instructional/teaching assistants, school community liaisons, parent advisers, parent advocates, or parent volunteers. They play a critical role in many aspects: They help parents navigate an unfamiliar school system. They help children make their initial adjustment to school and provide bilingual instructional support. They help teachers, speech and language specialists, and psychologists with assessment and testing. They interpret parent-teacher conferences. They translate forms, newsletters, and other written information. They help plan special cultural events. Regularly planned special cultural events, such as a Chinese New Year Parade, Heritage Day, or Diversity Week, are considered very important. They are ways of honoring the Chinese culture and addressing multiculturalism. They bring parents and the community together to share their proud heritage with the school, affirm students' cultural identities, and encourage bicultural development.

Parent Leadership Empowerment.

Another dimension of education leadership is empowering parents and community leaders to partner with school administrators in the decision-making process at the school board level. Parent-educator partnerships may be a new idea to the parents in the Chinese American community and a long process for the administrators to undertake. It may take a long time for some Chinese Americans to understand the American education system as well as the concepts of parent involvement, home-school collaboration, and parent-educator partnership building. It may take a long time for some parents to feel comfortable just getting involved in the classroom or participating as equal partners with teachers or other school personnel. Immigrant Chinese Americans are not particu-

larly active, politically or socially, especially initially. The traditional reverence toward learning and respect toward teachers implies deference and delegating all decisions to the professional educators.

Nevertheless, it is possible to empower parents and community leaders to partner with school leaders in formulating a vision, setting policies, and sharing governance. If an administrator is culturally proficient and has reached out to the community and networked with parents and community leaders, parents and community leaders more than likely will feel sufficiently at ease to get involved at the policy-making level. Culturally sensitive and insightful education leaders know that working with the Chinese American community may take a personal touch and an extra bit of guidance. Upon receiving personal phone calls of encouragement and some gentle prodding, those parents or community leaders with relevant interests and potential are likely to represent the community and partner with the administrators in policymaking and program governance. Success stories of Chinese Americans elected to school boards have emerged in recent decades, most notably in New York City and many districts in California.

Classroom Interactions

Student-Teacher Relationship and Interactions. Although the traditional formal and rigid student-teacher relationship has gradually relaxed in the last two decades, it does have varying degrees of influence on Chinese American students. For the shy, timid, introverted, or newcomer student, the relatively open and informal student-teacher relationship in American schools may appear to be chaotic, confusing, improper, and inappropriate. Chinese American students in general (and these

students in particular) tend to be quiet, passive, obedient, and overly respectful toward teachers and other school personnel.

These students can be put at ease by a warm (but not overwhelming) friendliness and sincerity, along with genuine kindness to and interest in them (Tinloy et al., 1988; Young & Lum, 1982). An open-door policy is helpful and welcoming to "hanging back" students (Tinloy et al., 1988). For older immigrant students, it may be necessary to explain that calling students or schoolmates by their first names (instead of their full names) is a common practice, while addressing a teacher as "Teacher," contrary to the Chinese practice, carries a somewhat impolite connotation in an American classroom.

Some students may feel considerable stress if attention is drawn to them in class (Feng, 1994). Some students may need extra time to become comfortable with compliments and/or learn how to respond to compliments appropriately. Thus, teachers may need to avoid putting students on the spot, in either positive or negative ways. Some students may be sensitive to school personnel calling them "honey" or "sweetheart" or "Miss/Mr. Last Name/Full Name." School personnel's casual physical contact, such as a friendly hug, may cause some uneasiness to older immigrant students. To sum up, it might be wise for school personnel to play things conservatively and go easy and slowly when acculturating immigrant students into the mainstream practices of interpersonal interactions.

Classroom Teaching-Learning Interactions. Coming from a tradition that stresses retention of knowledge via rote memorization and repetition, Chinese students need time adjusting to a teaching-learning approach that focuses on hands-on explorations, discovery, and discussions. Older students new to an American classroom may

need help with give-and-take interactions. Extra attention at the start, such as individualized encouragement, being offered opportunities to succeed, a non-threatening atmosphere, and simple yes/no tasks will help build up a student's confidence (Young & Lum, 1982). Explaining the differences in class interaction is helpful. Newcomer students may need help understanding that raising one's hand to ask or answer questions and participating in class discussion is expected in the teaching-learning process, and is not an act of showing off. Another strategy is encouraging the buddy system and peer modeling. Some Chinese students may look to their peers for cues about the American way of classroom interactions (Tinloy et al., 1988). Encouraging students with leadership skills to subtly provide peer support and peer modeling may be a way to help some students.

Accommodating Learning Styles. As discussed in the learning style section of this chapter, Chinese children tend to exhibit a highly reflective response style (Kitano, 1980), appear to be visually oriented (Wu, 1982; Young & Lum, 1982) and field-dependent (Zhang & Carrasquillo, 1995), and prefer a systematic, structured teaching-learning approach (Wu, 1982). Thus, they need, and will take, a relatively long time to respond to questions. Offering a visual reinforcement of an oral exercise with a written handout or a summary of discussion is highly recommended. To accommodate Chinese students' tendency to depend on the teacher for guidance and their inclination to seek approval from the teacher, clearly spell out and explain specific and detailed guidelines or procedures, preferably in writing, as well as the outcomes expected, at the beginning of an assignment. These guidelines may need to be reiterated during exploration or discussion exercises.

Written guidelines or procedures also can help students structure their attention and keep their focus. In addition, you may need to assign both individual and group tasks. Meanwhile, Chinese students' relatively weak ability in and disposition toward verbal expression merits special attention. Involving students in fun oral exercises and meaningful, purposeful communicative interactions can promote the use of language and help improve communication skills (Cheng, 1995). In sum, teachers need to be observant, use their professional discretion, and apply a specific or a wide repertoire of instructional techniques to match the cognitive styles of their Chinese American students.

Counseling

Acculturation is believed to be a major moderator of the counseling attitudes and experiences of Asian Americans in general, and the Chinese in particular (Leong, 1986; Uba, 1994). According to Leong and Gim-Chung (1995), highly acculturated Chinese Americans are more likely to use traditional Western-based counseling services and require relatively little modifications to the Western counseling approaches, while middle-acculturated Chinese Americans usually need considerable modifications. Low-acculturated Chinese Americans need drastic modifications or completely different approaches. As such, the following implications and recommendations will focus on counseling medium- and low-acculturated Chinese American students.

Indirect Service Approach. Chinese American students, especially immigrant students of medium and low acculturation, often are reluctant to take advantage of counseling services. School personnel, however, must look for signs of the students' emotional stress. These students may

be facing the multiple tasks of acculturation and overcoming language barriers, as well as pressures from peers, parents, and academics. The stigma associated with mental illness, as well as cultural and language barriers, are factors that prevent them from seeking support. To help these students, an indirect service approach that targets less sensitive areas, such as academic and vocational counseling, or that focuses on physical health, can help them with "coincidental" psychological problems (Leong & Gim-Chung, 1995). Building rapport and offering culturally relevant and appropriate services, preferably by bicultural and bilingual professionals, is also helpful. Owing to the fact that bilingual and bicultural counselors are not easily available, ways to infuse Chinese cultural literacy through the application of specific strategies and techniques pertinent to counseling Chinese American students will be briefly described below.

Culturally Appropriate and Responsive Counseling. When talking about their innermost feelings, most people feel more at ease opening up to someone of the same cultural and linguistic background. Language barriers notwithstanding, in a study designed to investigate the differences between culturally responsive and culturally neutral counselors, students rated culturally responsive counselors significantly more expert, attractive, and trustworthy (Zhang & Dixon, 2001). Besides integrating the cultural values, beliefs, and attitudes of Chinese Americans into actual interventions, counselors may need to pay special attention to communication styles. For example, counselors need to know that it may be difficult to engage Chinese American students. They may appear reticent, avoid eye contact, and only respond to questions with brief replies and little or no elaboration.

Tactfully probing and asking questions will facilitate dialogue. Counselors also need to know that the trust-building process takes a long time. They have to be flexible and willing to be physically and emotionally available. Furthermore, counselors need to treat each student differently, according to his or her unique situation and needs.

Partnership-Building With Parents

Besides shared decision-making and governance, there are many other aspects of partnership-building at the classroom and the school site levels, as well as in terms of parent-teacher or parent-school staff collaboration. Because of the diversity of Chinese American parents and educators' familiarity with the more acculturated Chinese American parents, the discussion below will focus on information and strategies pertaining to collaborating with new immigrant parents.

Cultural Literacy and Self-Reflection.
Cultural literacy is not to be overlooked. Moreover, an understanding of Chinese American parents' perceptions of parental involvement is a must. Prior to involving parents, educators should examine their own values, beliefs, and feelings about Chinese American parents and their involvement in the classroom or at the school. With some self-reflection and a knowledge base about Chinese American parents and their views on home-school collaboration, educators then can design a support system and devise specific strategies to accommodate the needs of Chinese American parents in building partnerships.

A Support System To Build Partnerships.
Just as a bilingual and bicultural support system is needed for effective leadership, a support system with a designated office and staff is needed for coordinating parent partnership-building, especially for school districts or programs with sizable Chinese

American student populations. Although the focuses are slightly different, both systems aim at linking school and home and, therefore, they can and should overlap. Please refer to the administration and leadership section for leadership support information. For general support regarding parent partnership-building in the classroom or at the school level, a discussion follows.

The long-term goal of the parent partnership-building staff is to advocate for equal partnerships and coordinate parent-partnership building. Initially, the partnership-building office may simply help parents navigate the education system and assist with all school-related issues. Gradually, the designated office and staff need to establish a network with community-based organizations and the Chinese language media to provide bilingual information about the school system, disseminate translated newsletters informing parents about upcoming events or updating regular activities, and develop parent handbooks and resource directories. To serve as ambassadors to link the parents and community, some of the designated staff members obviously need to be bilingual and bicultural. Establishing a support system to build partnerships with parents is not a new concept. Many school districts in California have invested in such support systems and have seen steady improvement in parent collaboration.

Language and Culture Barriers.
Limited English proficiency often leads to feelings of confusion, awkwardness, inadequacy, and inferiority. Immigrant parents commonly cite language barriers as one of the main factors inhibiting their participation in their child's schooling. However, language differences should not be interpreted as deficits that create barriers to a parent's involvement in school. If a support system is not available at the district level, due to a

small number of Chinese American students, oral interpretation and written translation still can be offered to parents. Bilingual parent or community volunteers, para-educators and other school personnel, or a three-way telephone interpreting service (offered by phone companies) can facilitate oral communication. Translating newsletters, parent handbooks, and other written information is another strategy. Immigrant parents with more formal education probably prefer translated written information (Lee, 1995), usually keeping the written documents for future reference. Parents with more education generally have had some English background and prefer to take their time reading the written communication with the help of a dictionary.

Newcomer parents, regardless of English proficiency, may need help overcoming cultural barriers concerning parent involvement as well. Educators may have to help them understand that parent involvement is highly desired or even required in American schools. The concept of parent collaboration or partnership-building as an integral part of the American school system is contrary to the perception of interfering or "checking on" the teacher commonly held in the homelands.

Another barrier is older children's inhibitions. Some older children are embarrassed or ashamed of their parents' accents, limited education, or poor English, and thus they discourage their parents from becoming involved at school. As Huang (1993) states, parent involvement should be cultivated in a way that not only enhances schooling but also reduces tension in the family. Educators need to convey to parents that they value and support the various forms or levels of involvement and contributions by parents and other family members at home, at school, or in the community.

Personal Touches and Connections.

Personal touches are extremely helpful in getting Chinese American parents, especially reticent ones, to come forward and get involved. Personal touches and connections take various forms and styles. They include, but are not limited to, warm welcomes, personal greetings, personal contacts, face-to-face invitations, personal notes, phone calls, and home visits. Personal touches also can be expressed in attitudes, such as a willingness to be flexible to accommodate a parent's schedule and a meeting location. Personal touches not only break down the invisible yet formidable barrier between parent and school personnel, but also give parents a feeling of being honored by educators, whom they look up to with respect.

Personal touches send a powerful message. They manifest school personnel's willingness to go above and beyond in efforts to reach out to parents. They also manifest school staff's professional dedication to giving personal attention to each and every parent. As a result, parents feel invited to join in rather than imposed upon. This positive feeling then leads to a sense of obligation to reciprocate. In return, parents become more willing to come forward and get involved, to collaborate with educators, and to become school partners.

Chapter 5
Health, Mental Health, and Health Care

Health Concepts and Beliefs   **90**
   Views of Physical Health   **90**
   Concept of Mental Health   **91**
   Views on Promoting and Maintaining Health   **91**
Interpretations of Causations of Physical and Mental Illnesses   **92**
   Pluralistic Assumptions of Causes of Illnesses   **92**
   Multiple Suppositions of Causation of Mental Illnesses   **92**
Healers and Healing Approaches   **93**
   A Pluralistic Healing System   **93**
   Folk Treatments   **93**
   Folk Nutrition   **94**
      Food Groups and Dietary Therapy   **94**
      Tonics and Vitamins   **95**
   Traditional Chinese Medicine   **95**
      Treatment Modalities and Diagnoses   **95**
      Chinese Herbal Medications   **96**
      Chinese Medicine Treatment Procedures and Techniques   **97**
   Supernatural Health Care and Treatments   **97**
Issues Related to Pluralistic Healing Approaches   **98**
Mental Health Healing   **99**
Oral Hygiene and Dental Heath   **99**
Postpartum Care   **100**
Sexuality   **101**
Death and Dying   **102**
Implications for Health Care Professionals   **103**

Health Concepts and Beliefs

Views of Physical Health

The Chinese views of health and illness are strongly influenced by the Chinese polytheistic belief systems; Confucianism, Buddhism, Taoism, and Animism all play a role in shaping Chinese people's health beliefs. Although the Chinese perceptions of health and illness are linked to these beliefs, the traditional notion of health and illness is based on the theory of the yin and yang forces and the five elements fundamental to Taoism (Chan, 1998; Salimbene, 2000; Tang & Park, 1999). Confucian teaching preaches that the body is the physical linkage between generations and therefore is to be kept healthy, not injured or abused. Buddhism views sickness as an inevitable part of suffering in life caused by desires and retributions for wrongdoings. Therefore, symptoms of illness should be ignored as part of the attempt to expunge desire, and medical inter-vention is sought only after personal and folk healing approaches have failed (Kaiser Permanente National Diversity Council, 1999). Meanwhile, influences of Animistic beliefs ascribe malevolent spirits with the power to cause illnesses and supernatural beings with the magical powers to restore health.

Taoism provides a comprehensive conceptualization of fitness and well-being, nutrition, etiology of illness, diagnosis, and treatment. In Taoism, the concept of health or illness is rooted in the belief of equilibrium between the two opposite but complementary cosmic forces of yin and yang and the corresponding conditions of "cold" and "hot." The goal is to achieve a state of harmony between humanity and the universe by flowing in accordance with nature. A person in good health is in tune with the cycle of the seasons, the climate, the land, the family, the people around him or her, and with his or her inner self. His or her flow of *qi (chi)*, or vital energy, inside his or her body is steady, smooth, and without obstruction. On the other hand, any deficiencies or excesses of physical, spiritual, social, or natural elements can cause an imbal-ance or disharmony, which in turn results in illness. This conceptualization of the flow of qi and its importance is reflected in the traditional fitness programs of *qigong (Qi Gong, Chi Gong, or Chi Kung)* and *taiqi (Tai Chi, tai chi)*. Both exercise regimens focus on gentle and flowing movements, accompanied by meditation and breathing exercises, to promote and regulate the flow of qi.

More specifically, yin is the female, negative, or passive force, associated with darkness, coolness, dampness, and emptiness. Yang is the masculine, positive, or active force, associated with light, heat, dryness, and fullness. Yin is believed to restore energy, while yang protects the body from intrusion by foreign forces. Any imbalance in the content or the flow of these forces will result in unhealthy conditions. To restore health, balance has to be reestablished by medication that centers on yin yang therapy or by acupuncture. For more than 2,000 years, Chinese medical practices have utilized this yin yang theory to diagnose and treat most illnesses. Excessive "heat" or yang illnesses include symptoms of fevers, dehydration, ear infections, cold sores, and skin eruptions. "Cold" or yin maladies are believed to be caused by intrusion of cold or "bad wind." Wind refers to airborne agents, such as drafts and germ-carrying air, and is considered the cause of infectious ailments (e.g., measles), coughing, headaches, diarrhea, as well as other, more serious, diseases like cancer. In accordance with the yin yang conceptualization, the Chinese classify foods into hot and cold groups, and a balanced diet means moderate consumption of both food groups to maintain or restore the equilibrium of yin and yang forces (Chan, 1998; Hoang & Erickson, 1982, 1985; Kaiser Permanente National Diversity Council, 1999; Lee, 1989; Lee, D'Alauro, White, & Cardinal, 1988; Matocha, 1998; North East Medical Services, 1994; Salimbene, 2000).

Concept of Mental Health

The mind is not separated from the body in the Chinese conceptualization of health. In other words, the body and the mind are considered one entity, functioning together as a unit. This holistic view implies that wellness occurs when physiological and psychological functions are harmoniously integrated, manifesting a healthy equilibrium of the yin and yang forces as well as the smooth and steady flow of qi. Mental health and psychiatric treatments are fairly new concepts, imported from the West along with the introduction of Western medicine at the beginning of the last century. Traditionally, psychological ailments, such as abnormal behaviors, depression, and other psychological disorders, are expressed in psychosomatic terms and interpreted as symptoms of an imbalance of the yin and yang forces and/or a lack of harmony of emotion. In summary, disturbance of the

yin and yang balance and excessive emotion that disrupts the flow of the qi are perceived as being directly linked to a person's physical and psychological health.

Views on Promoting and Maintaining Health

In accordance with this conceptualization of health, "moderation" and "regularity" are the key words in maintaining and promoting holistic physical and mental fitness and wellness. Keeping fit and staying healthy entails a balanced intake of hot and cold food groups and regularity of elimination. Foods in the extremely hot or cold categories may be consumed, but in moderation. Emotion must be regulated to keep oneself in balance. Excessive emotions are to be avoided. Physical activities are encouraged, but need to be done in moderation and with regularity. Traditional exercises, such as taiji (Tai Chi) and qigong (Chi Gong), are practiced because they are not strenuous and are mild forms of exercise. Both taiji and qigong focus on concentration, meditation, and breathing exercises to promote and regulate the flow of qi.

It is believed that with the smooth flow of qi running through the body and the mind, disturbing thoughts and harmful elements (caused by excessive yin or yang forces trapped inside the organs) can be expelled. Thus, regulation of the flow of qi helps correct the imbalance of the yin or yang force, promotes the steady flow of a balanced qi, and ensures the total well-being of body and mind.

Both Chinese health conceptualization and health practices operate from a polytheistic perspective. Pluralistic interpretations of causes of sickness, simultaneous utilizations of contrasting health care approaches, and multiple healers are characteristics of Chinese medical care and health practices.

Further discussions of the etiology of illness and health practices are described below.

Interpretations of Causations of Physical and Mental Illnesses

Pluralistic Assumptions of Causes of Illnesses

The blended Chinese folk belief system of Confucianism, Buddhism, and Taoism permeates all aspects of Chinese lives from birth to death, as well as their worldview, including that of health and illness. This unique folk belief system, combined with Animism and Western medicine, forms the pluralistic theoretical bases from which assumptions of causes of physical and mental illnesses are derived.

Urban and educated Chinese, including most Chinese Americans, understand basic Western science and accept the notion that germs, bacteria, viruses, genetics, malnutrition or poor diet, lack of exercise, depression, and environmental factors are disease-causing agents. In the meantime, they generally also embrace some folk beliefs and supernatural beliefs. Examples of folk beliefs of possible causes of illness include getting wet or chilled, hot-cold food intake imbalance, violating cultural taboos, and stress or excessive emotions. Supernatural beliefs identify divine punishment for sins or moral transgressions, curses, spells, soul loss, evil spirits, displeased ancestors, and bad *fengshui* (*Feng Shui*) or geomancy as the causes of illnesses. It is reasonable to state that the more educated the Chinese American, the less likely he or she will believe in supernatural causes. Chinese Americans from a more rural and less educated background, on the other hand, are more likely to adhere to the animistic and supernatural beliefs to a greater degree.

Multiple Suppositions of Causations of Mental Illnesses

The Chinese holistic view of health believes that wellness occurs when psychological and physiological functions are harmoniously integrated. One should, therefore, simultaneously consider the state of the mind and the state of the body. Chinese suffering from psychological problems often express their conditions in the form of psychosomatic symptoms, and thus complain about headache, loss of appetite, indigestion, dizziness, or fatigue, and they seek relief from professionals who heal physical ailments (Chan, 1998; Uba, 1994). Consequently, behavioral abnormalities and psychological disorders are interpreted as symptoms of imbalance between yin and yang or a discordance in harmony of emotions. The causes of mental disorders are primarily attributed to biological and supernatural factors, although natural factors, psychological issues, and the individual's own attributes are also believed to contribute to the problem to a much lesser degree. Biological factors include hereditary flaws and an imbalance of yin and yang forces. Implicated supernatural factors include all of those discussed previously, involving the ancestors, spirits, gods, deities, and demons, as well as the timing and circumstances of birth and fengshui. Soul loss, a curse, or a divine punishment for sins of parental or ancestral moral transgressions are most frequently cited as the reason for a mental problem. Meanwhile, Chinese people also ascribe other mental health ailments to natural factors, such as environmental pollutants, psychological issues of stress, depression, or guilt associated with immoral behaviors. Individual factors of personality and emotional attributes also are considered

(Chin, 1996; Kaiser Permanente National Diversity Council, 1999; Matocha, 1998; Tang & Park, 1999; Uba, 1994).

Healers and Healing Approaches

A Pluralistic Healing System

Chinese people will seek health information and medical intervention from a variety of sources, including family members, Western doctors, Western pharmacists, traditional Chinese herbalists, traditional Chinese medicine doctors and acupuncturists, folk healers, ancestors, clergy, shamans, spirits, and gods. Speculation about the cause of the ailment determines which person (or persons) or supernatural beings will be asked to intervene. Often, people will employ a blend of Western, traditional Chinese, folk, and supernatural approaches and practices. A holistic approach also is emphasized. Traditionally, the focus is on the well-being of the whole body rather than on treatment of a localized area of the body or the immediate relief of a condition. In other words, the goal is the restoration of equilibrium—the harmonious balance of the yin and yang forces and the steady flow of the qi (Chan, 1998; Hoang & Erickson, 1982; Lee, 1989; Matocha, 1998).

Traditional Chinese herbalists, Chinese medicine doctors and acupuncturists, folk healers, Buddhist and Taoist priests, and shamans may not be readily available in smaller Chinese communities in the United States. In communities with a larger Chinese population, these healers offer their services in independent clinics or even inside larger Chinese supermarkets. They often advertise their businesses in the Chinese-language media. In recent years, they have received more recognition as credible sources of alternative medicine; major private and government-subsidized health insurance even authorize coverage for consultation with and treatment by such health providers. In smaller communities, where there is no Chinese medical doctor or Chinese herbalist, a small, over-the-counter collection of non-prescription Chinese medicine often is available in most Chinese grocery stores. Self-diagnosis and self-medication is a fairly common practice for minor ailments. Folk healers (often, family members or friends) and shamans do not set up shop for business; they usually are known in the community and are referred by word-of-mouth. Buddhist and Taoist clergies offer consultation and provide spiritual healing to patients upon request, and patients may come from all directions, as a congregation for a Buddhist or a Taoist temple is not well-defined.

Inasmuch as this book is aimed at helping educators and service providers gain insight in working with Chinese children and families, a brief discussion of folk healing approaches and practices, folk dietary practices, and Chinese traditional medical practices will follow. Although Western health care and medical practices will not be described, readers are to be reminded that Chinese Americans, for the most part, seek medical treatments and health healing from Western physicians more than from any other source. Western healing practices generally are taken alone or in conjunction with folk practices, traditional Chinese medical practices, and spiritual healing.

Folk Treatments

Like most people in the world, the Chinese routinely use home remedies passed down from generation to generation as the first recourse at the onset of a symptom. Home-spun curative treatments utilized by the Chinese consist of a therapeutic diet of hot-cold food therapy; special tonics, drinks, or herbs; and avoidance of cultural taboos. Such folk treatment modalities as therapeutic massages and therapeutic steam baths may be administered. Folk treatments can be self-administered or administered by another person, and entail simple techniques learned by observation rather than formal training.

Therapeutic massage, also called "scratching the wind" by some Chinese, is a dermabrasive technique widely used to treat "wind illnesses" such as fevers, headache, heat stroke, cold, and coughing. It can be self-administered or administered by a family member, and it may or may not include using medicated or mentholated ointment such as Tiger Balm (a eucalyptus-based oil) or Ben Gay. The technique involves abrading the skin with a harmless edge (such as that on a coin or a spoon) on the forehead, bridge of the nose, neck, thorax, chest, and back to release the "toxic wind," or the excessive, unhealthy air currents trapped inside the body. Self-pinching (without using a coin or a spoon) also can be done by using the thumb and the index finger, or the index finger and the middle finger, to pinch the skin over the aforementioned areas. Dermabrasive massages usually produce bruises, welts, or "whip markings" that last for several days and often lead to misunderstandings and investigations of child or spousal abuse (Chan, 1998; Kaiser Permanente National Diversity Council, 1999; Salimbene, 2000).

Therapeutic steam baths and cupping are other folk treatments, although not widely used. Breathing the pungent herbal vapor produced from the steam provides temporary relief for common colds with high fever. Cupping can be done by a folk healer or a traditional Chinese doctor. This technique involves pressing heated cups firmly upon the afflicted areas or acupuncture points to relieve muscle pain or congestion (Kalman, 1989).

In the United States, home remedies of various forms of dietary therapy (therapeutic hot-cold food diet, special herbal medicinal diet, special tonics) and avoidance of cultural taboos are likely to be practiced more than the folk practices of therapeutic massage and therapeutic steam baths. Newly arrived immigrants have been observed using home remedies and folk treatments more often than acculturated immigrants do.

Folk Nutrition

Food Groups and Dietary Therapy. The Chinese think that diet plays a critical role in regulating, promoting, and restoring health. Many preventive and curative measures rely on dietary regulations. The Chinese dietary beliefs and practices are based on the Taoist classification of food groups. Foods and beverages are basically classified as either "hot" or "cold" in terms of attributes or properties based on yin and yang theory. This conceptualization suggests that food, upon consumption and digestion, will either heat up the body or cool it down. Examples of hot foods include alcohol and other stimulant beverages, fatty and preserved foods, spices, and some tropical fruits. Illnesses derived from consumption of hot foods are constipation, dysentery, nasal bleeding, upset stomach, or blisters. Hot foods have the therapeutic effect of curing illnesses caused by over-consumption of foods in the cold group. Cold foods include, but are not limited to, seaweed, some seafood, oranges, sugarcane, coconuts, plums, lotus seeds, beans, and cold liquids. Cold foods may cause indigestion, diarrhea, and upset stomach, but can be curatives for illnesses caused by hot foods.

In addition to the basic classification of hot and cold, foods are also placed in secondary groupings of the allergic group, the moderate group, and the nourishing group. The allergic group of foods, such as some seafood and exotic foods, may cause allergies and skin problems. The moderate group is considered benign and neutral in terms of hot and cold properties, and includes fish, pork, moderate climate fruits, and most vegetables. Foods in the nourishing group are believed to be especially beneficial during times of illness, convalescence, and old age. These foods include lotus seeds, chicken broth, shark fins, bird's nest (swallow's saliva), Chinese dates, and ginseng. Chinese folk nutrition advocates a balanced intake of hot and cold food along with consumption of moderate food.

Therapeutic cuisine can be either a folk practice or a prescription by a traditional Chinese medicine doctor. When a patient is on a therapeutic diet, strict adherence to a regimen of exclusion and abstinence of certain food groups and intake of the prescribed group are enforced. Cultural or folk taboos also impose dietary restrictions and inclusion of specific foods during pregnancy, postpartum, or convalescence (Chan, 1998; Lee, 1989; Lee, D'Alauro, White, & Cardinal, 1988; Salimbene, 2000; Tang & Park, 1999). Some of the restrictions may be therapeutic in nature to restore balance of yin and yang. While some suggestions about consuming specific foods may have sound nutritional merit, some are merely superstitious practices or old wives' tales.

Tonics and Vitamins. Chinese people are believers in the benefits of consuming tonics or highly nourishing foods during convalescence and old age, as well as during fall and early winter. It is believed that certain tonics and/or foods have special medicinal potency and nourishing value that can supply or replenish the nutrients needed for recovery, boost the energy level, promote overall health, or help weather the winter months. Special dishes are prepared with medicinal herbs for the elderly, the weak, or the whole family. This cultural practice of taking nutritional supplements remains alive in America to a limited extent. Chinese restaurants in cities with a large Chinese American population advertise their specialties in Chinese newspapers every fall. At home, it is not unusual to see expensive ginseng tea or overcooked ginseng in chicken or pork broth being served to the elderly or the weak over a long period of time, or on a regular basis if the family can afford it. Ginseng roots of different varieties are readily available in Chinese medicine stores or grocery stores. In fact, it is a Chinese immigrant from Taiwan who cultivated wild American ginseng in Wisconsin and built a thriving business selling American ginseng domestically and in East and Southeast Asia. Taking vitamin supplements has become a common practice among children and adults of some urban middle class families in China, Taiwan, and Hong Kong. Chinese American elders, however, are more slowly becoming accustomed to taking vitamin supplements, as many of them still prefer ginseng and traditional herbs. Younger Chinese Americans are more likely to take vitamins instead of ginseng, the traditional tonics, or other medicinal herbs.

Traditional Chinese Medicine

Treatment Modalities and Diagnoses.
Besides using home remedies and folk healing practices, Chinese Americans have been known to consult trained professionals specializing in traditional Chinese medicine (Hoang & Erickson, 1982, 1985). Traditional Chinese medicine includes the treatment modalities of herbal and dietary therapies, acupuncture, acupressure, and moxibustion. The focus of these traditional Chinese

medicine practices is not on combating the disease, but rather on restoring, maintaining, and enhancing health. Consequently, the diagnostic and treatment procedures are very different from Western practices. Compared to the extensive and invasive procedures of examinations and laboratory tests of Western medicine, which often are aided by instruments and machines, the approach undertaken by a traditional Chinese medical doctor is very simple. Diagnosis is made by closely inspecting the patient's eyes, tongue, and skin color of the face and hands, inquiring about the symptoms and health history, and feeling the pulse. Pulse diagnosis is considered the best tool and may be used alone without looking at the patient's eyes or skin color. A trained and experienced physician can tell the condition of the humors and vital organs simply by feeling the pulse. Abdominal palpation is occasionally used as well (Tom, 1989, cited in Chan, 1998; Matocha, 1998).

Chinese Herbal Medications.

The more frequently and widely used traditional treatment prescribed by the traditional doctor is herbal medication. Herbal remedies may be prepared and consumed as medication or as part of daily meals. However, the preparation of herbal medication is cumbersome and time-consuming, as a large amount of water is added to the herbs and the mixture is cooked for several hours to allow the liquid to concentrate. Nowadays, limited herbal extracts in pill form are available. Besides herbs, traditional Chinese medications also include such natural substances as fine clay and insects, animal body parts, or even small whole animals. Animals and animal byproducts used for Chinese medicine include seahorses, snakes, seashells, turtle shells, deer antlers, bear gallbladders and spleens. Many of these medications are based on sound pharmacological principles and many of them have been validated by Western laboratory research. Some of the traditional Chinese medications, however, have little or no pharmacological properties. Some of them even have been found to contain a high level of harmful chemical compounds (Kaiser Permanente National Diversity Council, 1999). Some are banned from being imported into the United States or the Federal Drug Administration has issued warnings of their possible dangers. News of

such warnings appears in the Chinese media every now and then.

Chinese Medicine Treatment Procedures and Techniques. Besides herbal medications, traditional Chinese medical treatments also employ the techniques of acupuncture, acupressure, and moxibustion to treat a variety of illnesses, such as arthritis, heart problems, some forms of cancer, and conditions involving acute pain. Acupuncture is a procedure of painlessly inserting fine, sterilized needles into vital pressure points of the body to regulate, promote, or restore the steady and harmonious flow of qi and maintain a homeostatic condition within the body. Acupuncture often is accompanied by acupressure, a technique of applying physical pressure to acupuncture points. Moxibustion is the technique of burning herbal medications and applying the heated substance to the torso, neck, or sometimes the site of the acupuncture before or after the needle has been inserted (Matocha, 1998; Salimbene, 2000). Moxibustion is intended to add further therapeutic stimulus when it accompanies acupuncture. Acupuncture and moxibustion may be administered alone, although supplementary herbal medications and/or dietary therapy often are prescribed as well. Acupuncture is used to cure a variety of ailments, relieve pain, and anesthetize patients for surgery (Kalman, 1989).

Supernatural Health Care and Treatments

The animistic belief in the supernatural etiology of illness has been quite influential among Chinese people, especially regarding mental illness. Animistic preventions and treatments have been practiced for a very long time, most likely before written history. Less educated and older Chinese Americans with rural backgrounds are particularly inclined to believe in animistic and supernatural powers. Supernatural or spiritual healing practices are sought either before turning to, or in conjunction with, Western medicine (Chin, 1996; Hoang & Erickson, 1985). Prevention measures derived from spiritual and supernatural beliefs include performing good deeds; adherence to prescribed societal codes of conduct; avoidance of cultural taboos; paying respect and making offerings to ancestors, spirits, deities, and gods on a regular basis; wearing or hanging amulets; and ensuring good fengshui. Supernatural remedies to restore health include ritualistic offerings and animal sacrifices, prayers or chants, exorcism, soul calling, drinking or sprinkling the patient with holy water, and correcting or rearranging fengshui.

Some of the treatments or interventions may require the help of a broker, such as a priest or a shaman, who performs the rituals or negotiates with ancestors or spirits. A more severe ailment may require an elaborate ritual, which usually is performed by a priest or a shaman. It is also a common practice to have the patient or a family member communicate directly with ancestors or the supernatural beings. Simpler rites can be performed to appease the spirits and to seek intervention by praying, burning incense and spirit money (fake bills for the deceased ancestors to use in the yin world), sacrificing animals, and making votive offerings.

When seeking intervention from supernatural powers, usually more than one approach is utilized. Ancestors are most often consulted, along with other deities and fengshui masters. Younger Chinese American families may not know the specific details or the proper rituals to solicit spiritual intervention. They may enlist an overseas relative to help, requesting spiritual and supernatural healings from abroad.

Issues Related to Pluralistic Healing Approaches

As mentioned earlier, home remedies, self-medication (using over-the-counter drugs), folk practices, and supernatural healings are utilized to various degrees, depending on the level of acculturation and availability of the healers, medications, and resources. For the most part, Chinese Americans favor Western medicine. However, traditional medicine and traditional Chinese doctors are still highly regarded, especially among the older generations and more recent immigrants. For example, Chinese Americans rushed to buy Chinese herbs for preventing and treating Severe Acute Respiratory Syndrome (SARS). Before there were any confirmed SARS cases in San Francisco or the immediate vicinity, two particular types of herbs merely believed to possibly prevent and treat SARS sold out completely within a few days in San Francisco's Chinatown (Lan, 2003).

Older adult immigrants often prefer to consult both Western and Chinese medicine doctors, although they may delay seeing a Western doctor until the condition becomes critical. It is believed that some illnesses are better treated by traditional medicine, while others are better treated by Western doctors. For example, Western medicine and procedures are considered by many to be more effective for the immediate relief of high fevers or acute pain, and for surgery, dentistry, eye problems, heart attacks, and strokes. Traditional treatments are considered superior for treating joint and muscle injuries, arthritis, lumbago, asthma, chronic illnesses, and some forms of cancer (Salimbene, 2000; Tang & Park, 1999).

Because Western treatment works well for faster symptomatic relief, a Western doctor may be consulted first for diagnosis and immediate treatment. Once the diagnosis is determined, the patient may follow the prescribed treatment completely or partially (Salimbene, 2000; Tang & Park, 1999). The prescribed medication may be taken as directed for only a few days and then discarded as soon as the symptoms have abated, as some Chinese Americans may not understand the necessity of finishing the medication for the entire prescribed duration. Compared to the more natural herbal medicines, Western medications are perceived to be very potent and more fitting for physically bigger Westerners. This perception, coupled with the concern about medications' side effects, sometimes leads Chinese Americans, especially seniors and new immigrants, to reduce the dosage of their prescriptions (Chan, 1998). Some older Chinese Americans, concerned about the disturbance of the body's balance that might result from relying on Western medication and treatment, use traditional herbal medicines to counteract the imbalance, not being aware of any possible complications or negative interactions (Tang & Park, 1999).

Traditional methods of Chinese healing generally are sought as an alternative treatment if the Western treatment does not bring quick relief, if a negative or pessimistic prognosis is given, or if surgery or chemotherapy is advised. Often, the traditional treatment may replace or be used along with the Western treatment. The patient or the family may not disclose the use of traditional treatment to the Western physician for fear of arousing disapproval or giving offense (Matocha, 1998; Salimbene, 2000). Moreover, Chinese Americans will typically turn to folk practices of nutritional therapy and supernatural practices before seeking Western or traditional treatment, or in conjunction with

Western treatment. They also tend to seek consultation from several contrasting sources and take several forms of treatment. While supernatural or spiritual healing generally is not harmful to the ailing body, the folk dietary therapy may contradict dietary guidelines prescribed by the Western doctor.

Mental Health Healing

The holistic view of traditional Chinese medicine does not distinguish mental illness from physical illness. Even today, no traditional Chinese medicine doctor specializes in mental healing. Psychiatric treatment only became available when Western medicine was introduced. As a result, consultants and healers for mental health have basically the same training as those specializing in physical health. The Chinese generally are not ready to recognize a mental health problem, and thus either deny the existence of the problem or delay seeking help to deal with a mental disorder.

The Chinese consider having a mental health problem shameful and a disgrace that should be kept within the family. This tremendous sense of embarrassment results in guilt that affects not only the patient but also the family. Traditional values emphasize self-control, self-reliance, perseverance through adversity, and reliance on the family. Revealing private concerns or familial problems to outsiders and seeking extra-familial intervention for the resolution of personal problems are considered especially embarrassing and shameful. Furthermore, Chinese people do not think talking about a problem will help solve problems, and some Chinese believe that mental disorders are divine punishments meted out for immoral behavior by the patients or their families. Consequently, such coping strategies as self-discipline, willpower, attention

diversion, and Taoist and Buddhist fatalistic acceptance and endurance are promoted (Chan, 1998; Matocha, 1998; Tang & Park, 1999; Uba, 1994). This reluctance to seek help sometimes leads to misconceptions about intervention. Some Chinese firmly believe that therapy is futile, while others even think the therapist will make them "crazy" (Uba, 1994).

Disharmony of yin and yang forces is perceived to be the root of psychological problems. Somatic interpretation of the symptoms and holistic perception of the body, mind, and emotions, along with the cultural factors discussed above, are the major factors inhibiting the recognition and treatment of a mental problem. If treatment is sought, it is usually oriented toward biological and supernatural treatment. Due to limited availability of houses of worship and/or clergy or shamans, unfamiliarity with the rites, and other factors, Chinese Americans sometimes ask overseas relatives to perform long-distance spiritual rituals or other supernatural healing practices for the patient.

Oral Hygiene and Dental Health

Many early childhood educators and teachers have noticed the poor condition of Chinese American children's oral health. Some preschoolers show very severe symptoms of baby tooth decay, to the extent that they have to wear dental caps on their teeth. This problem is brought on by having a bottle in bed, having too much starchy and sugary food, and not brushing the teeth. This phenomenon reveals the bigger problem of the Chinese people's negligence in oral hygiene. Although oral hygiene is mentioned and promoted in health education in school, little effort is put forth at school to teach and practice the correct way to brush teeth. As a result, many Chinese do not develop a habit of brushing their teeth correctly. Contemporary parents do teach and monitor their children's tooth brushing at home, but their own method or modeling may be less than ideal. It is probably fair to say that nearly all Chinese people brush their teeth first thing in the morning, but not everyone repeats the brushing before bedtime. Some urban and more educated mothers have only started to brush their toddler's or preschooler's teeth in the last decade or two. Even so, not every mother does it correctly. Flossing is a very new concept and very few people floss regularly. Few foreign-born Chinese American parents 30 years or older knew about dental floss while growing up.

Many Chinese only go to the dentist when they have a severe toothache or need to have major dental work done. Regular dental checkups and cleanings rarely take place in Taiwan or China, and there is little treatment for dental problems in traditional Chinese medicine. According to the yin and yang theory, a toothache is considered a manifestation of excessive yang forces. The most a traditional Chinese doctor can do is prescribe herbal medications to calm or cool the body, which does not really bring immediate relief or provide a cure. Therefore, the Chinese believe in the superiority of Western dentistry.

Chinese Americans, especially those who have dental insurance, have learned to pay more attention to oral hygiene and dental health. They are more likely to have routine checkups and clean and brush their teeth twice a day. Nonetheless, many could improve their oral hygiene habits, including proper tooth brushing, regular flossing, and brushing toddlers' and preschoolers' teeth.

Postpartum Care

Although parturition is a natural part of a woman's life, postpartum care traditionally has been considered critical and is taken very seriously. Due to blood (a yang force) loss associated with parturition, a postpartum woman's equilibrium is viewed as severely out of balance; thus, special care is needed to restore the yin and yang harmony. Even nowadays, many well-educated Chinese and Chinese American women strongly believe in the importance of postpartum care. It is believed that proper postpartum care can boost the overall health of the mother, and, consequently, benefit the baby. On the other hand, inadequate care will result in chronic problems, such as arthritis for the mother. Furthermore, as discussed in Chapter 6 (Disabilities and Intervention), what a mother does or eats during postpartum is viewed as directly contributing to a child's genetic defect or disability (Chin, 1996).

Called "doing the month" or "sitting the month," the postpartum woman is not supposed to venture out for a month after giving birth. She is to be confined inside the house to prevent exposure to cold, wind, and airborne agents (Lee, 1989; Lee, D'Alauro, White, & Cardinal, 1988). Except for when she is breastfeeding her baby, the mother is excused from all chores and encouraged to rest. If she has an older child or other children, her involvement and interaction with them during the month is very limited. A female elder, usually a family member, provides postpartum and baby care, and assumes control of all the mother's chores.

During this period, measures of folk taboos and dietary regulations are imposed and reinforced. While there are minor regional variations of folk taboos and dietary restrictions, the focus generally is on avoiding cold and wind and prohibiting the intake of cold liquid and cold foods (in terms of both temperature and properties). Instead, a diet regiment heavy on hot food groups and special tonics is emphasized. Some women still avoid most fruits and vegetables (they are considered too cold for the already cold body) and/or suspend bathing, showering, and hair washing until the bleeding has ceased.

As with many traditional practices, postpartum care has been undergoing modifications to accommodate societal changes and modern life. Many Chinese American women do not follow the full-fledged rituals for postpartum care, mainly because they do not have a female family elder around, they are not knowledgeable enough about the details of the care procedures, and they do not have access to all the ingredients for the special diet or tonics.

In communities with a high concentration of Chinese Americans, however, services are available on a fee-for-service basis. Middle-age women may offer individualized in-home service to moms and babies for a while. The hired hand provides much the same services that a female family elder does, so that the mother can rest and receive the care she and her baby need. Fashioned after postpartum care businesses in the homelands, such as in Taiwan, centers for "sitting the month" have sprung up in the last decade. Chinese newspapers carry advertisements for such services. Upon leaving the hospital, both mother and baby stay in their own room at the center (usually a big house) and receive the care they need. Folk taboos are observed and a traditional postpartum diet is served. For those who have access to it, such a service or business is very welcome as the mother and the baby are well taken care of, the mother gets much-needed rest and gets support from other mothers, and the rest of the family can sleep through the night.

Sexuality

Both Confucian and Buddhist traditional teachings urge women to be reserved and modest. Emotional regulation is indicative of proper upbringing, and public display of strong emotion is discouraged. Although adherence to these notions is changing quite rapidly, expressions of affection and physical contact between opposite genders in public are still considered inappropriate. Typically, families avoid frank discussions about sexuality, either between parent and child or between friends of the same gender. By and large, the culture's sexual values are more conservative. Although the incidence of premarital sex and divorce are on the rise in China, Hong Kong, and Taiwan, they are still far from being as common as in the United States. Premarital sex is still considered immoral, although it has become more common and more acceptable. Divorce is legal but not encouraged or well-accepted. Chinese society usually attributes marriage failure to the wife and is cruel to divorced women.

Homosexuality is slowly being discussed openly in Taiwan, but to a much lesser degree in China, where homosexual relationships are illegal in many parts of the country and homosexuals may be subjected to severe punishments. For the most part, homosexuality is considered abnormal and immoral and varying degrees of shame and stigma are associated with it. The shame and stigma the family have to endure often are tremendous, while the person who is gay is overwhelmed with guilt for putting the family in the situation. In a society where clear-cut traditional sexual roles are expected and reinforced, the obligation to continue the family line and take care of the ancestors' spirits continues to be strong. As the number of children decline, the pressure on a son to produce an heir has become more acute. Perhaps due to the traditional, long-standing gender inequities, male homosexual couples seem to be more open and active in promoting the social acceptance of their sexual orientation than female homosexuals, who seem to be more fearful of becoming openly gay. Homosexual Chinese Americans, either gay or lesbian, certainly find American society to be much more open and receptive. Their parents, consequently, tend to be more understanding and receptive.

Death and Dying

Despite the fact that death, from the Buddhist perspective, is viewed as a natural part of the life cycle, the Chinese have a tendency to avoid talking about death or referencing death-related subjects for fear of inviting death. The influence of this practice is so profound that many Chinese avoid buying life insurance or preparing a will. The number four (and 14, 40, etc.) is the superstitious unlucky number, just like the number 13 is in the West, because it sounds similar to the word for "death." Patients and their families generally shun symbolic connotations associated with death, such as room four or the color white (the color of mourning). When faced with a terminal illness and death, the patient or the family may not want to talk about it frankly or openly. Consequently, many patients die before bidding farewell to loved ones or fulfilling a last wish.

The holistic belief in the union and interaction of the body and mind suggests that hurtful bad news received by the mind is harmful to the body and might speed up death's arrival (Chan, 1998; Kaiser Permanente National Diversity Council, 1999). The family may prefer that the patient not be told about a terminal condition, or they may prefer to tell the patient themselves. The dying individual also may prefer to delegate the decision-making to the family. Some Chinese believe dying at home will bring bad luck. Others believe that the spirit may get lost and can't find its way home if death occurs in a hospital (Chan, 1998; Chin, 1996). When someone dies, extended family members and friends visit the home to mourn the deceased and console the immediate family. Such objects as amulets, jewelry, and favorite items of the deceased or their paper replicas, and spirit money (fake bills) are placed inside the coffin to send the deceased off to the yin world. The accompanying objects are much like luggage someone carries when traveling or moving to a new place.

Mourning rituals and periods have been simplified and shortened to accommodate modern life styles and job demands, both in the homeland and in America. Burial and cremation are preferred and practiced most widely in the United States. When the dead are properly buried or cremated, remembered, honored, and worshiped in ancestral worship, it is expected that their benevolent spirits will protect and bless the living family members. If not, their errant spirits will turn evil and dangerous, and can possess vulnerable children or adults and cause illness or misfortune. Children, especially those who die before reaching puberty, usually are buried or cremated in a simpler ceremony. They usually are not honored or worshiped afterwards for fear of bad luck, although they remain dear to their parents' hearts. While attitudes are changing, most Chinese Americans do shun the practices of organ donation or autopsy. It is believed that the dying need to have an intact body, with all of the body parts and organs, in which the soul will reside in the yin world.

Implications for Health Care Professionals

Although a handful of health care facilities on both coasts of the United States offer bilingual and culturally competent health care services to Chinese American patients, the availability and accessibility of these types of services are still extremely limited. While health care professionals are eager to provide optimal and culturally sensitive services to their clients, there is a dearth of literature regarding culturally appropriate ways for providing health care to Chinese Americans. The Internet provides limited information; the best resource appears to be a booklet called "A Provider's Handbook on Culturally Competent Care: Asian and Pacific Island American Populations," published in 1999 by the Kaiser Permanente National Diversity Council. Most of the following information is derived from this booklet, from other sources, and from personal insights:

- It is essential to build relationships and establish trust between the caregiver and the patient and the family. While the caregiver may give task completion precedence over spending time interacting with the patient, a seemingly rushed appointment may lead the patient and/or the family to draw negative conclusions about the care and the caregivers, and will affect their decisions about how they would follow up with the diagnosis and/ or treatment. Spending time to establish a personal rapport, especially during the first visit, may prove fruitful. Chinese patients and families appreciate a caring professional's continued interest and genuine concern (Tang & Park, 1999).
- Health care professionals would benefit from an understanding about Chinese health concepts and a holistic view of treatment. The Chinese etiology of illness is linked to the polytheistic belief system, and the conceptualization of the interconnectedness of the mind, body, and spirit dictates a holistic approach to treatment. Mainstream professionals and health care providers may not be familiar with these complex and drastically different orientations and views. A basic understanding would help the professionals break down barriers and better understand the patient's cultural background.
- While prescribing Western forms of treatment, inquire about what other forms of treatment the patient may be undertaking. Providers may be able to complement the treatment, or caution against using those folk, traditional, or supernatural methods of treatment that would be contraindicated in conjunction with Western medicines.
- Blood loss, even a small amount, is believed to disrupt the humoral or yin and yang balance within the body. Therefore, surgery is often shunned for fear of loss of blood and loss of soul.
- Cultural sensitivity in communication and social interaction must be heeded, especially when the contact involves seeking help. Indirect styles of communication are particularly suitable for Chinese Americans. Face-saving is extremely important to the Chinese. Disclosure of personal or family problems to an outsider puts the family reputation at risk. Sensitivity can be shown by avoiding a hasty and frank discussion of the patient's problem before a relationship is established (Tang & Park, 1999).
- More traditional Chinese American patients and families may view health care professionals as authority figures who provide absolute answers and solutions to the patient's problems. This respect for professionals' authority is further reflected

in a number of ways, including avoiding questions or making a patient's needs explicit, as well as by withholding critical comments. Unfortunately, this well-intentioned desire to show respect often results in failure to seek explanation of the nature of illness, treatment options and procedures, and prognosis (Tang & Park, 1999). Meanwhile, health care providers who somehow do not live up to the expected images of an authority figure are perceived quite differently. Health care professionals who are relatively nondirective, maintain a neutral and nonjudgmental demeanor, and do not offer decisive or absolute solutions may be perceived as uncaring or even incompetent (Uba, 1994).

- For treating mental disorders, it is important to understand the immigration and acculturation experience, as well as the collective Chinese American identity premised on the family and community. Treatment efforts may need to include the family's input.

- A consideration of spirituality or supernatural forces and their effect on the patient and the family must be recognized. Western psychotherapy sometimes is criticized for lacking a spiritual element, which is considered critical from the Chinese perspective.

- The Kaiser Permanente National Diversity Council (1999) maintains that some mental health therapy approaches have proven particularly suitable with Asian and Pacific Island patients. Its report recommends a focus on external stress (versus internal conflicts), direct problem-solving techniques, active problem management (versus problem discussion), and external instead of internal solutions (p. 61).

- An interpreter may help ensure the patient or family's comprehension of medical information and terminology. It is also sometimes important to have a cultural broker to help bridge the cultures, especially when folk, spiritual, or supernatural healing treatments are involved.

Chapter 6
Disabilities and Intervention

Views of Disabilities **106**
Causation of Disabilities **106**
　　Random Events **107**
　　Genetic/Hereditary Reasons **107**
　　Medical Factors **107**
　　Pregnancy and/or Postpartum Behaviors **107**
　　Supernatural Factors **108**
　　　　Divine Punishment **108**
　　　　Demonic Possession **108**
　　　　Ancestral or Fengshui Factors **108**
Perceptions and Attitudes Toward Intervention **108**
Help-Seeking and Intervention **109**
Collaboration With Professionals **109**
Implications and Recommendations **110**
　　Concept of Developmental Services and Special Education **110**
　　Cultural and Linguistic Interpreters **111**
　　Relationship-Building, Trust, and Face-Saving **111**
　　Communication and Interaction Styles **112**
　　Parental Gratitude and Reciprocity **112**
　　Formality, Courtesy, and Other Cultural Considerations **112**

Views of Disabilities

The Chinese consider a child not only an individual but also an extension of the parents and the product of many generations. This perception of the parent-child relationship profoundly affects the parental view of a child's disability. Reactions to the discovery that a child has a disability may include not only shock but also guilt and shame. Many Chinese believe that children with disabilities show physical evidence of their handicaps. Therefore, they think only physical disabilities need treatment (Bebout & Arthur, 1992; Matsuda, 1989). Conditions that are not physically discernible, such as mild learning disabilities, speech impairments, and emotional disorders, are perceived to be a result of laziness or oppositional behavior. Thus, parents may not see the need for any intervention in such cases (Bebout & Arthur, 1992). They may believe that such developmental problems are the result of improper training on their part, and will experience particular guilt and shame. If the disabilities are more severe, then the parents may feel a strong sense of social shame or stigma. This stigma, for the most part, is associated with the perceived causes (Chan, 1998).

Professionally speaking, the division of disabilities into many subcategories is a fairly new conceptualization in Taiwan and China. Although special schools for the blind, deaf, and mute have existed for decades, special education professionals were not aware of, or did not recognize, more specialized divisions of special education programs. Academic investigation and practical applications, in terms of identification, assessment, and service delivery, were not available until very recently. Even today, some of the special education terminologies used are not always consistent or well-defined (some special education pundits often include original English terminology in parentheses to alleviate confusion), not to mention well-understood. Besides the belated development of investigation and application, other factors exist that impede the recognition of needs and the delivery of services. Because of sociocultural and language differences, in addition to the lack of valid and reliable instruments for identification and assessment, reading disability was not officially recognized until 1977 and services were not provided until 1983 in Taiwan (Chang, 1992; Chang, Hung, & Tzeng, 1992). A similarly slow pattern in the distinguishment and recognition of subcategories of special education, as well as in providing services, existed in Mainland China with a slightly later starting date.

Causation of Disabilities

As Chan (1998) points out, many of the beliefs and suppositions about the causation of disabilities mirror the attributions of the etiology of illness (previously described in the chapter on health). Readers may find it helpful to refer to that section to gain a more global understanding of the Chinese perspective of illness and disabilities. The causes of disabilities most commonly cited by Chinese Americans can be classified into five major categories: random events, genetic factors, medical factors, maternal behaviors, and supernatural factors.

Random Events

Most educated and urbanized Chinese Americans more or less acknowledge and accept the reality that a child's birth defect or disability is merely a random event. They generally recognize that it is something that occurs, and that often there is little explanation as to why it happens. Believers of the random event theory may or may not also take other considerations into account, including environmental factors such as pollution or the proximity of electromagnetic fields. Since finding scientifically conclusive evidence to pinpoint the exact cause is no easy task, a random event is more or less accepted as the main explanation for the cause of birth defects or disabilities. Parents who accept the random event theory generally are more inclined to seek intervention and collaborate with professionals.

Genetic/Hereditary Reasons

Contrary to the supposition of random happenings is a belief in genetic disorders or heredity flaws as being the cause of birth defects. This explanation usually derives from observing discernible types of hereditary physical or mental disabilities. However, mild forms of hereditary defects or disabilities may not be easily recognized and consequently are often ignored or neglected. The failure to acknowledge mild forms of hereditary conditions or disabilities often results in parents blaming the child for being lazy or behaving deviously.

Medical Factors

Medical factors are also attributed as the cause of disabilities. Disease and prenatal or perinatal traumas can result in problems and are easily recognized and blamed as the causes.

Although a medical factor may be found as the cause, the reason as to why it happened to the child is the subject of various speculations. Please refer to the detailed etiology of illness in the section on health.

Pregnancy and/or Postpartum Behaviors

Some Chinese Americans ascribe a more socioculturally oriented explanation of a birth defect or a disability. What a mother did or ate during pregnancy and/or postpartum is considered a direct link to a genetic defect (Chin, 1996). The mother is seen at fault, and hence blamed for her presumed failure to follow prescribed dietary and health care practices and/or folk beliefs about avoiding certain taboos.

There are many regional varieties of folk dietary prescriptions and restrictions, as well as behavioral taboos, during pregnancy and/or postpartum. For example, one mother attributed her child's Down syndrome to her failure to drink enough beef soup during pregnancy (Chan, 1998). Some Chinese hold a traditional belief that pregnant women should avoid using sharp objects, such as scissors, for fear of causing a congenital hand anomaly or cleft palate (Chan, 1998; Tinloy et al., 1988).

If the mother accepts the assumed cause of the problem, she most likely feels a strong sense of guilt and is prone to self-blame. If, on the other hand, she does not agree with the superstition but is being blamed for causing the problem, she is likely to be in denial and extremely resentful. This supposition of genetic defect reflects a traditional belief in the significance of so-called "womb rearing," which advocates that the expectant mother engage the unborn fetus in "prenatal education" by maintaining a calm mood, engaging her mind, and adhering to the societal code of conduct.

Supernatural Factors

Another category in the presumed etiology of disabilities is related to supernatural forces. Supernatural influences on the Chinese are very strong, and supernatural beliefs permeate many aspects of Chinese life. While Chinese Americans, compared to rural or less educated Chinese in the home-lands, generally are not ardent believers in supernatural forces, the residual effects of their supernatural beliefs can still sway their interpretation of what causes disabilities to occur. Birth defects and/or disabilities often are attributed to divine punishment from a higher being, demonic possession of the child's soul, displeased ancestors holding grudges, or bad fengshui that interferes with the flow of fortunes.

Divine Punishment. A disability may be considered a punishment for sins or moral transgressions committed by either the parents or the ancestors. Such divine punishment is also known as a curse or a vengeance. Such attribution often leaves the parents with a strong sense of embarrass-ment, shame, self-blame, guilt, and stigma. These charged emotions sometimes lead parents to adopt a fatalistic, passive attitude, thereby perceiving the disability as the "karma" or the fate of the child. Conse-quently, they may stoically accept the situation and make little or no effort to seek intervention. On the other hand, parents may actively appeal to the supernatural power for a cure. They may employ reli-gious, spiritual, or other supernatural practices to atone for perceived wrongdoings.

Demonic Possession. Related to divine punishment is an animistic belief in demonic possession, or the belief that a disability is caused by malevolent demons, ghosts, or evil spirits that occupy the child's soul. Parents who hold this belief may seek a spiritual or supernatural cure on their own

through prayers, meditation, offerings, and chants. Another method is to enlist the service of a shaman, priest, or a spiritual master to perform exorcisms or other healing rituals to drive the demon out of the body. Amulets also may be worn, or hung somewhere in or around the house for protection and warding off the malevolent spirits.

Ancestral or Fengshui Factors. One belief holds that errant or displeased ances-tors who were not properly buried or cremated, remembered, honored, or wor-shiped may hold a grudge and are seeking vengeance. Parents often try to make amends by pleading for forgiveness and appealing for a blessing during a ceremony. Bad fengshui, or the geomancy of the residence, the interior of a house, or the gravesite of the ancestors, is also believed to be a possible culprit of the misfortune. To remedy the situation and to prevent the misfortunes from worsening, a fengshui master may be consulted to recommend necessary changes or accommodations.

Perceptions and Attitudes Toward Intervention

Parental coping strategies and attitudes toward intervention are closely linked to their views regarding child-rearing practices and the etiology of disabilities. The extent of the influence of these two aspects on Chinese Americans is difficult to determine. It is reasonable to assume that new immigrants and more traditional Chinese Americans are more likely to hold a fatalistic point of view that the child's disability is the child's karma, and that little or nothing can be done to alter the karma. Hence, they tend to accept and endure the handicap as the way it is and believe they should take care of the child at home on their own. They may appear to be very passive in seeking intervention or in collaborating with an interventionist. Acculturated Chinese Americans, on the other hand, are more likely to hold perceptions and attitudes toward intervention similar to those of mainstream Americans.

Chinese parents believe in the notion of the age of innocence. Children too young for school generally are perceived as not yet being capable of understanding. As a result, parents tend to be overly lenient, tolerant, and indulgent (Bond & Hwang, 1986; Ho, 1989; Ho & Kang, 1984; Stevenson et al., 1992; Tang & Park, 1999). Deviant behaviors in young children are tolerated and any developmental delays or disabilities may be overlooked or ignored. Moreover, parents tend to be reluctant to seek outside professional help. The traditional value of self-sufficiency, coupled with the emphasis on "keeping the family shame inside the family," make seeking outside support the last resort. Concern about shame and loss of face further inhibits parents from seeking professional intervention until it is absolutely necessary. The shame and loss of face associated with the parental perception of their failure is two-fold—the perceived failure in taking care of their own family needs and their sense of failing in one's parenting roles and responsibilities.

Help-Seeking and Intervention

Educators should consider the perceptions and attitudes toward intervention discussed above when working with Chinese American children and families. Teachers and other interventionists also need to be aware that most Chinese Americans are eager to seek intervention for a child with special needs, especially those parents who are aware of the federal requirements for providing specialized and individualized education services. It is reasonable to state

that these parents recognize the limitations their children face but also want to seek professional services and support for them, thus enabling their children to reach their fullest potential. Parents who believe that random events, heredity, medical, or behavioral factors are the source of a disability are especially inclined to seek intervention and collaborate with professionals. Parents who believe in divine punishment, demonic possession, ancestral anger, or fengshui are still likely to seek professional intervention, as they also pursue their own supernatural interventions. For information regarding possible approaches of supernatural interventions, please refer to the section on Supernatural Health Care and Treatments in Chapter 5. Similar or identical supernatural approaches are employed for disabilities. Perception and attitude aside, other factors may interfere with parents seeking intervention or collaboration with professionals. Parents from rural or less Westernized areas, or parents who are in the United States illegally, may view interventionists with fear and distrust (Tinloy et al., 1988). This wariness is heightened by the language barrier and unfamiliarity with or lack of awareness about available services.

Collaboration With Professionals

Culture and tradition dictate that parents assume an orientation of deference, noninterference, and delegation when interacting with professionals (Chan, 1998; Uba, 1994). While parents understand and believe it is their role and responsibility to teach and train their children at home, many parents think they should let the professionals take charge at school and make all the professional decisions for their child. They believe that they, as parents, should not interfere with professionals, deferring to their expertise and trusting that they know what is the best for their child. Many Chinese Americans, especially recent immigrants, are not aware of or familiar with legislative mandates and policies regarding developmental services and special education, such as Individualized Family Service Plans (IFSP) and Individualized Education Plans (IEP). They find the concepts of parental rights, responsibilities, entitlements, advocacy, due process, and collaboration with professionals and agencies to be foreign, confusing, troublesome, and threatening (Chan, 1998). When asked to choose alternatives, some Chinese American parents may appear perplexed, decline to make choices, defer to the professionals, or try to second-guess which alternative will please the professionals the most (Chan, 1998; Tinloy et al., 1988).

New immigrants, less-educated parents, and parents who view professionals with fear and distrust are unlikely to initiate contact. When contacted by a school or an agency, they may exhibit behaviors that mainstream interventionists consider non-involving or non-responsive. They tend to be quiet, polite, and attentive but passive. They ask few questions, volunteer little information, respond to questions with short answers, and make little or no effort to elaborate (Yao, 1988). When asked to collaborate, they usually will comply but may not completely follow through with any of the suggestions for involvement or reinforcement activities at home.

The high regard that Chinese American parents place on teaching personnel also may lead to their perceptions of professionals as authority figures. Although these views are changing, parents still expect teaching personnel to have the ultimate decision-making power. Parents may expect them to provide direct and highly prescriptive approaches, offer practical and concrete

assistance, and supply immediate and decisive solutions for a child's problems (Tinloy et al., 1988). If parents' high expectations are not met, they may consider the professional to be uncaring or incompetent. Subsequently, their credibility and respect diminishes.

Although intervention professionals may encounter some of the situations described above when interacting with Chinese Americans parents, in most cases they are likely to find working with Chinese American children and parents a very positive and rewarding experience. Chinese American parents, by and large, are eager to collaborate, pleasant to work with, and very supportive and appreciative of professionals.

Implications and Recommendations

Concept of Developmental Services and Special Education

As previously discussed, while some special education programs for handicapped children exist in Chinese American families' homelands, the division of some more specialized disciplines or areas of developmental services and special education is not recognized; thus, services are not yet available. In working with immigrant Chinese American parents, professionals first need to explain the concept of developmental services or special education and their related issues (Tinloy et al., 1988). To some parents, even special education for severely physically disabled children in a school setting is an alien concept, due to the unavailability of such services in Asia. On the other hand, some parents may not want to have their children in the special education program for fear of a perceived stigma associated with the disability. To alleviate parental apprehension, educators need to convey the values and benefits of the programs to the parents and establish trust. Additionally, the legislative mandates and policies regarding parental rights and responsibilities, as well as the roles and responsibilities of the service team members, need to be addressed. Few Chinese American parents are aware of, not to mention knowledgeable about, these issues. Even parents who have some knowledge about special education nevertheless may have many questions about the details of the legislative mandates and policies, the philosophy of recommended best practices, advocacy, and parent-professional collaboration. They also will be unfamiliar with a team approach that involves specialists from various disciplines, teachers, and paraprofessionals. The specific roles and responsibilities of each team member need to be explained to the family (Tinloy et al., 1988).

Cultural and Linguistic Interpreters

A bilingual and bicultural interpreter often is needed when professionals are explaining to parents about special education services. Sometimes, a bilingual family member or friend will serve as a language interpreter and a cultural broker. There are many advantages to this practice, including familiarity with the child and family, moral support, and interdependency (Chan, 1998). If the family does not have this resource, a skilled interpreter who is not only bilingual and bicultural but also knowledgeable about special education should be asked to help bridge the gap. In reality, this is not always possible. Professionals need to be creative in researching alternatives and soliciting or utilizing community resources. When utilizing community resources, it is imperative to ensure confidentiality and provide on-the-spot training.

Relationship-Building, Trust, and Face-Saving

Upon initial contact with the family, professionals need to immediately start working on building a trusting relationship and cultivating mutual respect. The basis for such a relationship can be developed by demonstrating sensitivity to linguistic and cultural issues, including culture-specific values and practices, as well as universal values of genuine care, concern, kindness, and dedication. It is crucial that professionals acquire culture-specific knowledge of traditional Chinese values, beliefs, and practices pertaining to religion, child rearing, health, mental health, and disabilities, as well as communication styles (Chan, 1998). In the mainstream American culture, professionals are often pressed for time, with heavy caseloads and strict accountability. As such, professionals tend to be task-oriented and cannot always attend to the details and subtleties that impact relationship-building, regardless of how well intentioned they are.

With the vast differences between the mainstream and the Chinese cultures in some areas, saving face may be overlooked by mainstream professionals, although not intentionally. Chinese American families, conversely, attach great value on sensitivity to issues of saving face, and they prefer taking an indirect approach to sensitive issues. Since families often experience guilt, shame, and stigma because of a child's disability, parents are particularly sensitive to protecting the family dignity and honor. They may not feel comfortable or ready to reveal information that is emotionally sensitive. Therefore, professionals are encouraged to spend time and make efforts to establish a solid parent-professional rapport. Interventionists are advised against venturing into frank and direct discussion of a specific problem too quickly (Chan, 1998). It may not sound professional, but it may be worthwhile to establish a casual and friendly personal relationship, in addition to a professional relationship, with the family. A casual and friendly chat about mutual or universal interests, such as family, food, or holidays, and discussion of unrelated information of parental interest are ways to make initial contact.

Communication and Interaction Styles

When communicating with the family, professionals need to remember the differences in Chinese styles of communication and interaction. The traditional virtues of emotional reserve and deference to authority inhibit some Chinese Americans from being assertive. Lack of familiarity with their legal rights and entitlements in the American special education system further prevents parents from pursuing developmental and special education services for their child. When contacted by an agency and provided with services, some parents may continue to act passive, submissive, or excessively dependent. In addition, other culturally prescribed behaviors may be manifested to convey respect. Interventionists may notice repeated head-nodding, smiling, avoidance of eye contact, refraining from asking questions or making needs explicit, and withholding information (Uba, 1994). Consequently, observing protocols, addressing child and family needs, reframing problems, and approaching parents in a circular and positive fashion holds out the possibility for greater input. Educators need to respect the family hierarchy and structure and value the family's decisions (Chan, 1998).

Parental Gratitude and Reciprocity

Parents' respect toward teaching professionals and service providers often evolves into a sense of deep gratitude and a moral obligation of reciprocity. Most Chinese American families are likely to feel a debt of gratitude toward the interventionists. Their gratitude may be displayed or conveyed through gift giving and invitations to special occasions. The parents, especially new arrivals, may give gifts of considerable monetary value, putting the interventionists in an awkward situation. A cultural broker might be needed to help untangle the dilemma. Generally speaking, professionals need to employ considerable tact and sensitivity in dealing with this reciprocity issue, because refusing to accept a gift or an invitation may be interpreted as rejection and failure to give face (Chan, 1998). Consequently, the delicate relationship and trust may be ruined and the damage to the relationship would be extremely difficult to repair. As a general rule, accept small gifts but explain to the family through a bicultural intermediary the reason why it is inappropriate for a professional to accept a valuable gift. If a professional believes that small gifts are given and accepted too frequently, he or she can return the favor by giving the child some small gifts. When going on home visits, it is customary for the family to offer drinks and/or refreshments; professionals are expected to take at least a few sips or bites.

Formality, Courtesy, and Other Cultural Considerations

Finally, a little cultural literacy pertaining to formality and courtesy will go a long way. While it is not essential, it is advantageous to pay a little more attention to some subtleties when interacting with families. It is also prudent to attend to formality. For example, it is wise to be conservative and dress somewhat formally and use more formal interaction and communication styles.

Informal dress, even for a home visit during warm weather, may be construed as a sign of disrespect and a lack of professionalism. Moreover, interventionists may find it beneficial to pay attention to culturally specific subtleties, such as greeting etiquette; acknowledging elders in the family; and receiving, exchanging, and offering food, drinks, gifts, or documents with both hands. Little details, such as significant colors and numbers, as well as body language and other nonverbal cues, also are important. For more information regarding these culturally specific subtleties, please refer to the Cultural Considerations and Communication Styles sections contained in Chapter 1.

References

Asakawa, K., & Csikszentmihalyi, M. (1998). The quality of experience of Asian American adolescents in activities related to future goals. *Journal of Youth and Adolescence, 27*, 141-163.

Bebout, L., & Arthur, B. (1992). Cross-cultural attitudes about speech disorders. *Journal of Speech and Hearing Research, 35*, 45-52.

Berndt, T. J., Cheung, P. C., Lau, S., Hau, K. T., & Lew, W. J. F. (1993). Perceptions of parenting in mainland China, Taiwan, and Hong Kong: Sex differences and social differences. *Developmental Psychology, 29*, 156-164.

Bond, M. H., & Hwang, K. K. (1986). The social psychology of the Chinese people. In M. H. Bond (Ed.), *The psychology of the Chinese people* (pp. 213-266). Hong Kong: Oxford University Press.

Bosrock, N. M. (1994). *Put your best foot forward: Asia.* St. Paul, MN: International Education Systems.

Buckley, L. C. (Comp.). (1997). *Asia and Southeast Asia language and culture profiles.* Sacramento, CA: California State University, Sacramento, International Studies Project at Sacramento.

Caplan, N., Choy, M. H., & Whitmore, J. K. (1992, February). Indochinese refugee families and academic achievement. *Scientific American, 266*, 36-42.

Chan, F., Lam, C. S., Wong, D., Leung, P., & Fang, X-S. (1988). Counseling Chinese Americans with disabilities. *Journal of Applied Rehabilitation Counseling, 19*(4), 21-25.

Chan, S. (1998). Families with Asian roots. In E. W. Lynch & M. J. Hanson (Eds.), *Developing cross-cultural competence: A guide for working with children and their families* (2nd ed., pp. 251-354). Baltimore: Paul Brookes Publishing.

Chang, F. (1973). *Responding to Chinese-American children.* San Francisco: Far West Laboratory for Educational Research and Development. (ERIC Document Reproduction Service No. ED 175979)

Chang, I. (2003). *The Chinese in America: A narrative history.* New York: Viking.

Chang, J-M. (1992, December). *A school-home-community-based conceptualization of LEP students with learning disabilities: Implications from a Chinese American study.* Paper presented at the Third National Research Symposium on Limited English Proficient Student Issues: Focus on Middle and High School Issues, Washington, D.C. Retrieved February 25, 2003, from www.ncela.gwu.edu/ncbepubs/symposia/third/chang.htm

Chang, J-M., Hung, D. L., & Tzeng, O. J. L. (1992). Miscue analysis of Chinese children's reading behavior at the entry level. *Journal of Chinese Linguistics, 20*(1), 120-159.

Chao, R. K. (1993, March). *Clarification of the authoritarian parenting style and parental control: Cultural concepts of Chinese child rearing.* Paper presented at the Biennial Meeting of the Society for Research in Child Development, New Orleans, LA. (ERIC Document Reproduction Service No. ED 361065)

Chao, R. K. (1994). Beyond parental control and authoritarian parenting style: Understanding Chinese parenting through the cultural notion of training. *Child Development, 65*, 1111-1119.

Chao, R. K. (1996a, August). *Reconceptualization of the authoritarian parenting style parenting and parental control: Some initial items.* Paper presented at the Biennial Meeting of the International Society for the Study of Behavioral Development, Quebec, Canada. (ERIC Document Reproduction Service No. ED 403015)

Chao, R. K. (1996b). Chinese and European American mothers' beliefs about the role of parenting in children's school success. *Journal of Cultural-Psychology, 27*, 403-423.

Chen, C. (1989). *A study of Chinese and American children's attitudes towards schooling*. (ERIC Document Reproduction Service No. ED 305165)

Chen, C., & Stevenson, H. W. (1995). Motivation and mathematics achievement: A comparative study of Asian-American, Caucasian-American, and East Asian high school students. *Child Development, 66*, 1215-1234.

Chen, C., & Uttal, D. H. (1988). Cultural values, parents' beliefs, and children's achievement in the United States and China. *Human Development, 33*, 351-358.

Chen, F-M., & Luster, T. (1999, April). *Chinese parenting reconsideration: Parenting practices in Taiwan*. Paper presented at the Biennial Meeting of the Society for Research in Child Development, Albuquerque, NM. (ERIC Reproduction Service No. ED 435480)

Chen, G-M. (1988, November). *A comparative study of value orientations of Chinese and American families: A communication view*. Paper presented at the Annual Meeting of the Speech Communication Association, New Orleans, LA. (ERIC Document Reproduction Service No. ED 300843)

Cheng, L-R. L. (1991). *Assessing Asian language performance: Guidelines for evaluating limited-English-proficient students*. Oceanside, CA: Academic Communication Associates.

Cheng, L-R. L. (1995). Service delivery to Asian/Pacific LEP children: A cross-cultural framework. In D. T. Nakanishi & T. Y. Nishida (Eds.), *The Asian American educational experience: A source book for teachers and students* (pp. 212-220). New York: Routledge.

Cheng, L-R. L. (1998). *Enhancing the communication skills of newly arrived Asian American students* (ERIC/CUE Digest No. 136). New York: ERIC Clearinghouse on Urban Education at Teachers College. (ERIC Document Reproduction Service No. ED 420726)

Cheng, L-R. L. (1999). Sociocultural adjustment of Chinese-American students. In C. C. Park & M. M-Y. Chi (Eds.), *Asian American education: Prospects and challenges* (pp. 1-17). Westport, CT: Bergin & Garvey.

Cheung, F. M. C. (1987). Psychopathology among Chinese people. In M. H. Bond (Ed.), *The psychology of the Chinese people* (pp. 171-212). Hong Kong: Oxford University Press.

Chi, M. M-Y. (1999). Linguistic perspective on the education of Chinese-American students. In C. C. Park & M. M-Y. Chi (Eds.), *Asian-American education: Prospects and challenges* (pp. 18-46). Westport, CT: Bergin & Garvey.

Chiang, L. H. (2000, October). *Teaching Asian American students: Classroom implications*. Paper presented at the Annual Meeting of the Midwestern Educational Research Association, Chicago. (ERIC Document Reproduction Service No. ED 447130)

Chin, P. (1996). Chinese Americans. In J. G. Lipson, S. L. Dibble, & P. A. Minarik (Eds.), *Culture & nursing care: A pocket guide* (pp. 74-81). San Francisco: University of California, San Francisco Nursing Press.

Chinn, T. (1967). *A history of the Chinese in America*. San Francisco: Chinese History Society of America.

Chiu, L. H. (1987). Child-rearing attitudes of Chinese, Chinese-American, and Anglo-American mothers. *International Journal of Psychology, 22*, 409-419.

Chung, W. (1997). Asian American children. In E. Lee (Ed.), *Working with Asian Americans: A guide for clinicians* (pp. 165-174). New York: Guilford Press.

Cultures of minority groups are gradually diminishing in Mainland China (in Chinese). (2003, November 9). *World Journal*, p. B2. Millbrae, CA: Author.

Crystal, D. S., Chen, C., Fuligni, A. J., Stevenson, H. W., Hsu, C., Ko, H., & Kitamura, S. (1994). Psychological maladjustment and academic achievement: A cross-cultural study of Japanese, Chinese and American high school students. *Child Development, 65*, 738-753.

Fejgin, N. (1995). Factors contributing to the academic excellence of American Jewish and Asian students. *Sociology of Education, 68*, 18-30.

Feldman, S. S., & Rosenthal, D. A. (1990). The acculturation of autonomy expectations in Chinese high schoolers residing in two western nations. *International Journal of Psychology, 25*, 259-281.

Feng, J. (1994). *Asian American children: What teachers should know* (ERIC Digest). Urbana, IL: ERIC Clearinghouse on Elementary and Early Childhood Education at the University of Illinois. (ERIC Document Reproduction Service No. 369577)

Fong, T. P. (2002). *The contemporary Asian American experience: Beyond the model minority* (2nd ed.). Upper Saddle River, NJ: Pearson Education.

Fuligni, A. J., & Stevenson, H. W. (1995). Time use and mathematics achievement among American, Chinese, and Japanese high school students. *Child Development, 66,* 830-842.

Gardner, H. (1989). *To open minds: Chinese clues to the dilemma of contemporary education.* New York: Basic Books.

Gardner, R. C. (1980, November). *Learning styles: What every teacher should consider.* Paper presented at the Rocky Mountain Regional Conference of the International Reading Association, Boise, ID. (ERIC Document Reproduction Service No. ED 198059)

Gorman, J. (1998). Parenting attitudes and practices of immigrant Chinese mothers of adolescents. *Family Relations, 47,* 73-80.

Gu, M. (2001, June). *The education for all in time of study.* Paper presented at the 2001 China-U.S. Conference on Education, Beijing, China.

Hall, E. T. (1977). *Beyond culture.* Garden City, NY: Anchor Press.

Hirschman, C., & Wong, M. G. (1986). The extraordinary educational attainment of Asian Americans: A search for historical evidence and explanations. *Social Forces, 65,* 1-27.

Ho, D. Y. F. (1986). Chinese patterns of socialization: A critical review. In M. H. Bond (Ed.), *The psychology of the Chinese people* (pp. 1-37). Hong Kong: Oxford University Press.

Ho, D. Y. F. (1989). Continuity and variation in Chinese patterns of socialization. *Journal of Marriage and the Family, 51,* 149-163.

Ho, D. Y. F. (1994). Cognitive socialization in Confucian heritage cultures. In P. M. Greenfield & R. R. Cocking (Eds.), *Cross-cultural roots of minority child development* (pp. 285-313). Hillsdale, NJ: Lawrence Erlbaum Associates.

Ho, D. Y. F., & Kang, T. K. (1984). Intergenerational comparison of child-rearing attitudes and practices in Hong Kong. *Developmental Psychology, 20,* 1004-1016.

Hoang, G. N., & Erickson, R. V. (1982). Guides for providing medical care to Southeast Asian refugees. *Journal of the American Medical Association, 248,* 710-714.

Hoang, G. N., & Erickson, R. V. (1985). Cultural barriers to effective medical care among Indochinese patients. *Annual Review of Medicine, 36,* 229-239.

Hsu, F. L. K. (1981). *American & Chinese: Passage to differences* (3rd ed.). Honolulu, HI: The University Press of Hawaii.

Hsu, J. (1985). The Chinese family: Relations, problems, and therapy. In W. S. Tseng & D. Y. H. Wu (Eds.), *Chinese culture and mental health* (pp. 95-112). Orlando, FL: Academic Press.

Huang, G. (1993). *Beyond culture: Communication with Asian American children and families* (ERIC/CUE Digest No. 94). New York: ERIC Clearinghouse on Urban Education at Teachers College. (ERIC Document Reproduction Service No. ED 366673)

Huang, K. (1991). Chinese Americans. In N. Mokuau (Ed.), *Handbook of social services for Asian and Pacific Islanders* (pp. 79-96). Westport, CT: Greenwood.

Huang, S-B. (2002, June 20). Chinese immigrants from Fujian Province challenge New York public schools. *World Journal.* Retrieved June 13, 2003, from http://216.239.39.100search?q=cache:VburJWwWzIIL:www.gothamgazette.com/citizen/july

Huntsinger, C. S., Huntsinger, P. R., Ching, W-D., & Lee, C-B. (2000). Understanding cultural contexts fosters sensitive caregiving of Chinese-American children. *Young Children, 55*(6), 7-12, 14-15.

Huntsinger, C. S., & Jose, P. E. (1997, March). *Cultural differences in parents' facilitation of mathematics learning: A comparison of Euro-American and Chinese-American families.* Paper presented at the Annual Meeting of the American Educational Research Association, Chicago. (ERIC Document Reproduction Service No. ED 410026)

Huntsinger, C. S., Jose, P. E., & Ching, W-D. (1994, June). *Ethnic differences in early math learning: A comparison of Chinese-American and Caucasian-American.families.* Paper presented at the Annual Symposium of the Jean Piaget Society, Chicago. (ERIC Document Reproduction Service No. ED 375940)

Huntsinger, C. S., Jose, P. E., & Larson, S. L. (1998). Do parent practices to encourage academic competence influence the social adjustment of young European American and Chinese American children? *Developmental Psychology, 34,* 747-756.

Huntsinger, C. S., Jose, P. E., Shutay, J., & Boelcke, K. (1997, August). *Achievement, activity choice, and self-perception from early to late adolescence.* Paper presented at the Annual Meeting of the American Psychological Association, Chicago. (ERIC Document Reproduction Service No. ED 414534)

Huntsinger, C. S., Larson, S. L., Krieg, D. B., & Balsink, D. (1998, April). *Mathematics and vocabulary development in Chinese American and European American children over the primary school years.* Paper presented at the Annual Meeting of the American Educational Research Association, San Diego, CA. (ERIC Document Reproduction Service No. ED 422445)

Huntsinger, C. S., Schoeneman, J., & Ching, W-D. (1994, May). *A cross-cultural study of young children's performance on drawing and handwriting tasks.* Paper presented at the Midwestern Psychological Association Conference, Chicago. (ERIC Document Reproduction Service No. ED 373889)

Jensen, A. (1973). *Educability & group difference.* New York: Harper & Row.

Kaiser Permanente National Diversity Council. (1999). *A provider's handbook on culturally competent care: Asian and Pacific Islander American populations.* Oakland, CA: Kaiser Permanente.

Kalman, B. (1989). *China, the culture* (The lands, peoples and cultures series). New York: Crabtree Publishing.

Kelley, M. L., & Tseng, H-M. (1992). Cultural differences in child rearing: A comparison of immigrant Chinese and Caucasian American mothers. *Journal of Cross-Cultural Psychology, 23,* 444-455.

Kitano, M. K. (1980). Early education for Asian American children. *Young Children, 35*(2), 13-26.

Kong, D. (2003, December 29). Mandarin influence grows among U.C. Chinese: The shift from Cantonese is felt even in San Francisco's Chinatown. *The Sacramento Bee,* p. A4.

Lan, G-Z. (2003, April 28). Presumptively effective on SARS, Chinese medicinal herbs selling briskly (in Chinese). *World Journal,* p. B1. Millbrae, CA: World Journal.

Lau, S., Lew, W. J. F., Hau, K. T., Cheung, P. C., & Berndt, T. J. (1990). Relations among perceived parental control, warmth, indulgence, and family harmony of Chinese in Mainland China. *Developmental Psychology, 26,* 674-677.

Lee, E. (1997a). Overview: The assessment and treatment of Asian American families. In E. Lee (Ed.), *Working with Asian Americans: A guide for clinicians* (pp. 3-36). New York: Guilford Press.

Lee, E. (1997b). Chinese American families. In E. Lee (Ed.), *Working with Asian Americans: A guide for clinicians* (pp. 46-78). New York: Guilford Press.

Lee, E. S., & Rong, X-L. (1988, May). The educational and economical achievement of Asian-Americans. *Elementary School Journal, 88,* 545-560.

Lee, F.Y. (1995). Asian parents as partners. *Young Children, 50*(3), 4-9.

Lee, L. C. (1998). An overview. In L. C. Lee & N. W. S. Zane (Eds.), *Handbook of Asian American psychology* (pp. 1-19). Thousand Oaks, CA: Sage Publications.

Lee, L. C., & Zhan, G. (1998). Psychological status of children and youths. In L. C. Lee & N. W. S. Zane (Eds.), *Handbook of Asian American psychology* (pp. 137-163). Thousand Oaks, CA: Sage Publications.

Lee, S. J. (1996). *Unraveling the "model minority" stereotype: Listening to Asian youth.* New York: Teachers College Press.

Lee, R. V. (1989). Understanding Southeast Asian mothers-to-be. *Child Birth Educators, 8,* 32-39.

Lee, R. V., D'Alauro, F., White, L. M., & Cardinal, J. (1988). Southeast Asian folklore about pregnancy and parturition. *Obstetrics and Gynecology, 71,* 243-246.

Lee, X. L. (2002, September 28). Chinese has become the second foreign language in the U.S. (in Chinese). *World Journal,* p. A2. Millbrae, CA: World Journal.

Leong, F. T. L. (1986). Counseling and psychotherapy with Asian Americans: Review of the literature. *Journal of Counseling, 33,* 196-206.

Leong, F. T. L., & Gim-Chung, R. H. (1995). Career assessment and intervention with Asian Americans. In F. T. L. Leong (Ed.), *Career development and vocational behavior of racial and ethnic minorities* (pp. 193-226). Mahwah, NJ: Lawrence Erlbaum.

Leung, E. K. (1997, November). *Acculturation gap and relationship between first and second generation Chinese-Americans.* Paper presented at the Annual Meeting of the Midsouth Educational Research Association, Memphis, TN. (ERIC Document Reproduction Service No. ED 416290)

Leung, J. J. (1991). *Some cultural differences in academic motivational orientations between American and Chinese students.* (ERIC Document Reproduction Service No. ED 366455)

Leung. J. J., Maehr, M. L., & Harnisch, D. L. (1993). *Some sociocultural differences in students' academic motivational orientations.* (ERIC Document Reproduction Service No. ED 357862)

Li, C. N., & Thompson, S. A. (1981). *Mandarin Chinese: A functional reference grammar.* Berkeley, CA: University of California Press.

Lin, C-Y. C., & Fu, V. R. (1990). A comparison of child-rearing practices among Chinese, immigrant Chinese, and Caucasian-American parents. *Child Development, 61,* 429-433.

Lin, H. (2002, July). *An interpretative study on four kindergarten teachers' education perspectives in Taipei.* Paper presented at the Third Pacific

Early Childhood Education Research Association Conference, Shanghai, China.

Lin, S. (1988). *Name your baby in Chinese*. Singapore: Heian International.

Liu, M-L. (2003, May 9). Twenty-nine Chinese American students named Presidential Scholars (in Chinese). *World Journal*, p. A8. Millbrae, CA: World Journal.

Liu, X. (1996). *Best Chinese names*. Singapore: Asiapac Books.

Lorenzo, M. K., Frost, A. K., & Reinherz, H. Z. (2000, August). Social and emotional functioning of older Asian American adolescents. *Child and Adolescent Social Work Journal, 17*, 289-304.

Ly, P. (2003, January 25). More Chinese Americans choose Christianity. *The Sacramento Bee*, pp. E1, E7.

Major, J. S. (1989). *The land and people of China*. New York: J. B. Lippincott.

Matocha, L. K. (1998). Chinese-Americans. In L. D. Purnell & B. J. Paulanka (Eds.), *Transcultural health care: A culturally competent approach* (pp. 163-188). Philadephia: F. A. Davis Company.

Matsuda, M. (1989). Working with Asian parents: Some communication strategies. *Topics in Language Disorders, 9*(3), 45-53.

Mau, W-C. (1997). Parental influences on the high school students' academic achievement: A comparison of Asian immigrants, Asian Americans, and white Americans. *Psychology in the Schools, 34*, 267-277.

Miller, G., Yang, J., & Chen, M. (1997). Counseling Taiwan Chinese in America: Training issues for counselors. *Counselor Education and Supervision, 37*, 22-34.

Miller, P. J., Wiley, A. R., Fung, H., & Liang, C-H. (1997). Personal storytelling as a medium of socialization in Chinese and American families. *Child Development, 68*, 557-568.

Mordkowitz, E. R., & Ginsburg, H. P. (1986, April). *Early academic socialization of successful Asian American college students* (Technical Report No. 143). Paper presented at the Annual Meeting of the American Educational Research Association, San Francisco. (ERIC Document Reproduction Service No. ED 280927)

New York City Board of Education. (1989). *Asian American concerns: The report of the chancellor's task force*. (ERIC Document Reproduction Service No. ED 376239)

Ning, W-Y. (2002, December 5). Six Chinese American students among the finalists of the Siemens Westinghouse Math, Science & Technology Competition (in Chinese). *World Journal*, p. A4. Millbrae, CA: World Journal.

North East Medical Services. (1994). Cultural issues in providing care to Asians and Pacific Islanders. In the Association of Asian Pacific Community Health Organizations (AAPCHO) (Ed.), *Asian & Pacific Islander health care delivery* (pp. 6-9). San Francisco: Author.

Pang, V. O. (1995). Asian American children: A diverse population. In D. T. Nakanishi & T. Y. Nishida (Eds.), *The Asian American educational experience: A source book for teachers and students* (pp. 167-179). New York: Routledge.

Peng, S. S., & Wright, D. A. (1994). Explanation of academic achievement of Asian American students. *Journal of Education Research, 87*, 346-352

Pikcunas, D. D. (1986). *Analysis of Asian-American early childhood practices and their implications for early childhood education*. (Viewpoints 120, Information Analysis 070). (ERIC Document Reproduction Service No. ED 274422)

Porter, J. (1983). *All under heaven: The Chinese world*. New York: Pantheon Books.

Ridley, C. P., Godwin, P. H. B., & Doolin, D. J. (1971). *The making of a model citizen in communist China*. Stanford, CA: Stanford University, the Hoover Institute Press.

Rushton, J. P. (1985). Differential K theory: The sociobiology of individual and group differences. *Personal and Individual Differences, 6*, 441-452.

Salimbene, S. (2000). *What language does your patient hurt in? A practical guide to cultural competent patient care*. Amherst, MA: Diversity Resources.

Schickedanz, J. A. (1995). Family socialization and academic achievement. *Journal of Education, 177*(1), 17-38.

Schneider, B., & Lee, Y. (1990). A model for academic success: The school and home environment of East Asian students. *Anthropology and Education Quarterly, 21*, 358-377.

Shen, W., & Mo, W. (1990). *Reaching out to their cultures: Building communication with Asian American families*. (ERIC Document Reproduction Service No. ED 351435)

Shiang, J. (1984). *"Heart" and self in old age: A Chinese model* (Paper from the Project on Human Potential). (ERIC Document Reproduction Service No. ED 254466)

Sim, S. C. (1992). Social service needs of Chinese immigrant high school students in New York City. *Asian American Policy Review, 3*, 35-54.

Siu, S-F. (1992a). *Toward an understanding of*

Chinese American educational achievement: A literature review (Report No. 2). Baltimore: Johns Hopkins University Center on Families, Communities, Schools and Children's Learning. (ERIC Document Reproduction Service No. ED 343713)

Siu, S-F. (1992b). How do family and community characteristics affect children's education achievement? The Chinese-American experience. *Equity and Choice, 8*(2), 46-49.

Siu, S-F. (1994). Taking no chance: A profile of a Chinese-American family's support for school success. *Equity and Choice, 10*(2), 23-32.

Siu, S-F. (1996a). *Questions & answers: What research says about the education of Chinese American children.* (ERIC Document Reproduction Service No. ED 400077)

Siu, S-F. (1996b). *Asian American students at risk: A literature review* (Report No. 8). Washington, DC: Center for Research on the Education of Students Placed at Risk.

Smith, S., & Freedman, D. G. (1983, April). *Mother-to-toddler interaction and maternal perception of child temperament in two ethnic groups: Chinese-American and European-American.* Paper presented at the Annual Meeting of the Society for Research in Child Development, Detroit, MI. (ERIC Document Reproduction Service No. ED 250084)

Soo-Hoo, T. (1999). Brief strategic family therapy with Chinese Americans. *The American Journal of Family Therapy, 27,* 163-179.

Stevenson, H. W., Chen, C., & Lee, S. Y. (1992). Chinese families. In J. L. Roopnarine & D. B. Carter (Eds.), *Parent-child socialization in diverse cultures: Advances and applied developmental psychology* (Vol. 15., pp. 17-33). Norwood, NJ: Ablex.

Stevenson, H. W., Lee, S. Y., & Stigler, J. W. (1986). Mathematics achievement of Chinese, Japanese, and American children. *Science, 231,* 693-699.

Stevenson, H. W., Stigler, J. W., Lee, S. Y., Lucker, G. W., Kitamura, S., & Hsu, C. (1985). Cognitive performance and academic achievement of Japanese, Chinese, and American children. *Child Development, 56,* 718-734.

Steward, M., & Steward, D. (1974). Observation of Anglo-, Mexican-, and Chinese-American mothers teaching their young sons. *Child Development, 44,* 329-337.

Stigler, J., Smith, S., & Mao, L. (1985). The self-perception of competence by Chinese children. *Child Development, 56,* 1259-1270.

Sue, D. W. (1981). *Counseling the culturally different.* New York: John Wiley.

Sue, D., & Sue, D. W. (1991). Counseling strategies for Chinese Americans. In C. C. Lee & B. L. Richardson (Eds.), *Multicultural issues in counseling: New approaches to diversity* (pp. 79-90). Alexandria, VA: American Association for Counseling and Development.

Sue, S., & Okazaki, S. (1990). Asian American educational achievements: A phenomenon in search for an explanation. *American Psychologist, 45,* 913-920.

Suzuki, B. H. (1980). The Asian American family. In M. D. Fantini & R. Cardenas (Eds.), *Parenting in a multicultural society* (pp. 70-102). New York: Longman.

Takaki, R. (1989). *Strangers from a different shore: A history of Asian Americans.* New York: Penguin Books.

Tan, A. (1989). *The joy luck club.* New York: Ivy Books.

Tang, G., & Park, Y. (1999). *The Chinese community in the United States* (The CCHCP Community Profile Series). Seattle, WA: The Cross Cultural Health Care Program.

Tinloy, M., Tan, A., & Leung, B. (1988). *Assessment of Chinese speaking limited English proficient students with special needs.* Sacramento, CA: California Department of Education.

Trueba, H. T., Cheng, L-R. L., & Ima, K. (1993). *Myth or reality: Adaptive strategies of Asian Americans in California.* Washington, DC: Falmer Press.

Tseng, J. (1994, Fall). *Chinese American students and parental relations.* Retrieved September 2, 2003, from http://modelminority/com.article131.html

Uba, L. (1994). *Asian Americans: Personality patterns, identity, and mental health.* New York: Guilford Press.

Vernon, P. E. (1982). *The abilities and achievements of Orientals in North America.* New York: Academic Press.

Wang, X. (Ed.). (1996). *A view from within: A case study of Chinese heritage community language schools in the United States.* Washington, DC: National Foreign Language Center.

Wang, X., Bernas, R., & Eberhard, P. (2002). Variations of maternal support to children's early literacy development in Chinese and American Indian families: Implications for early childhood educators. *International Journal of Early Childhood, 34*(1), 9-23.

Wolf, M. (1970). Child training and the Chinese family. In M. Freeman (Ed.), *Family and kinship in Chinese society* (pp. 37-62). Stanford, CA: Stanford University Press.

Wong, M. G. (1995). The education of white,

Chinese, Filipino, and Japanese students: A look a high school and beyond. In D. T. Nakanishi & T. Y. Nishida (Eds.), *The Asian American educational experience: A source for teachers and students* (pp. 221-234). New York: Routledge.

Wong, S-L. C., & Lopez, M. (1995). *California's Chinese immigrant students in the 1990s.* San Francisco: Many Cultures Publishing.

Wu, D. Y. H. (1985). Child training in Chinese culture. In W. S. Tseng & D. Y. H. Wu (Eds.), *Chinese culture & mental health* (pp. 113-134). Orlando, FL: Academic Press.

Wu, H. T. (1982). Appendix 9: Learning styles of Chinese children. In J. Young & J. Lum (Eds.), *Asian bilingual education teacher handbook* (pp. 121-127) (Office of Education Grant No. OEG-71-4409). Cambridge, MA: Evaluation, Dissemination, and Assessment Center for Bilingual Education.

Xiao, W. (2002, October 20). Chinese Americans are moving to the suburbs: Census 2000 reveals a new trend (in Chinese). *World Weekly,* pp. 12-15. Millbrae, CA: World Journal.

Yang, G-M. (2002, November 3). Chinese community heritage language schools conference starts today (in Chinese). *World Journal,* p. B2. Millbrae, CA: World Journal.

Yao, E. L. (1979, April). *School teacher's perception of child-rearing by the Chinese.* Paper presented at the National Association for Asian American and Pacific Education Conference, San Francisco. (ERIC Document Reproduction Service No. ED 181095)

Yao, E. L. (1985, February). Adjustment needs of Asian immigrant children. *Elementary School Guidance and Counseling, 19,* 222-227.

Yao, E. L. (1988, November). Working effectively with Asian immigrant parents. *Phi Delta Kappan, 70,* 223-225.

Yau, J., & Smetana, J. G. (1996). Adolescent-parent conflict among Chinese adolescents in Hong Kong. *Child Development, 67,* 1262-1275

Yee, B. W. K., Huang, L. N., & Lew, A. (1998).

Families: Life-span socialization in a cultural context. In L. C. Lee & N. W. S. Zane (Eds.), *Handbook of Asian American psychology* (pp. 83-135). Thousand Oaks, CA: Sage Publications.

Yeung, W. H., & Lee, E. (1997). Chinese Buddhism: Its implications for counseling. In E. Lee (Ed.), *Working with Asian Americans: A guide for clinicians* (pp. 452-463). New York: Guilford Press.

Young, J., & Lum, J. (1982). Appendix 6: Bridging the Asian language and cultural gap. In J. Young & J. Lum (Eds.), *Asian bilingual education teacher handbook* (pp. 97-106) (Office of Education Grant No. OEG-71-4409). Cambridge, MA: Evaluation, Dissemination, and Assessment Center for Bilingual Education.

Young, R. L. (1998). Becoming American: Coping strategies of Asian Pacific American children. In V. O. Pang & L-R. L. Cheng (Eds.), *Struggling to be heard: The unmet needs of Asian Pacific American children.* Ithaca, NY: State University of New York Press.

Yu, J-S. (2002, April 19). Immigrants from Mainland China constitute the second largest immigrant group after Mexicans (in Chinese). *World Journal,* p. A3. Millbrae, CA: World Journal.

Zhang, N., & Dixon, D. D. (2001). Multiculturally responsive counseling: Effects on Asian students' rating of counselors. *Journal of Multicultural Counseling Development, 29,* 253-262.

Zhang, R. (2001, June). The *classical poem education of Chinese children.* Paper presented at the 2001 China-U.S. Conference on Education, Beijing, China.

Zhang, S. Y., & Carrasquillo, A. L. (1995, Summer). Chinese parents' influence on academic performance. *New York State Association for Bilingual Education Journal, 10,* 46-53.

Zhao, Y. (2002, December 14). To their beloved dead, offerings by the living. *The New York Times.* Retrieved on December 15, 2002, from www.nytimes.com

Index

A

Academic achievement   43, 44, 44–45, 64–65, 71, 73–74, 75, 77
  Adademic difficulties   76
  Risk factors   76–77
Acupuncture. *See* Health: Healing approaches
Ancestral worship. *See* Belief systems
Animism. *See* Belief systems
Asian homelands   12, 66

B

Babysitters   42
Behavior. *See* Character traits
Belief systems   17–18
  Ancestral worship   19, 25
  Animism   20, 90
  Buddhism   18, 90, 92, 93
  Christianity   20
  Confucianism   17, 65, 71, 74, 75, 90, 92
  Islam   20
  Polytheism   19, 90
  Taoism   18, 90, 92, 93
Bicultural/bilingual   9, 59, 82, 83, 87, 111
Birth order   47–48
Body language. *See* Communication style
Buddhism. *See* Belief systems

C

Cantonese. *See* Language
Celebrations   19, 24–25, 83, 84
  Chinese New Year   24–25
Character traits   20, 44, 54, 70, 84, 88
  Humility   22
Chi. *See* qi
Children's roles and responsibilities   44–45
Chinese medical practices   90
Chinese New Year. *See* Celebrations
Christianity. *See* Belief systems
Co-sleeping   42, 53

Cohabiting. *See* Family structure
Communication style   21, 35–36, 44, 71, 102, 111, 112
  Body language   22
  Confrontation avoidance   21
  Humility   22
  Nonverbal communication   21
  Smiles   22
Community outreach   82
Confrontation. *See* Communication style
Confucianism. *See* Belief systems
Counseling   39–40, 86, 104
Cultural traditions   58–59, 79, 94, 103, 109
Cultural values   74–76, 82, 86, 87, 112
Curriculum   72

D

Death and dying   102
  Mourning rituals   102
Dental health   99
Disabilities   106–107
  Causation   106–107
Discipline   54, 56–57, 69
Divorce   33, 38

E

Economic opportunities   13
Education   43–44, 46–47
  Administration   81–82
  Classroom interactions   69–71, 84
  Educational values   64–65
  Extracurricular activities   47, 75, 81
    Music lessons   47, 81
    Sports   47
  Heritage language school   79
  In America   67
  In homelands   66, 68
  Learning styles   71, 85
  Parental involvement   78–79, 84, 87
  Parental responsibilities   65
  Teacher/school responsibilities   65–66

Emotional problems   39
Etiquette   26, 46
Exercise   91
Eye contact   26

F

Family discord   38–39, 48–49, 55
Family expectations   37–38
Family interactions   35–37
Family structure   30–32
   Cohabiting   30–31
   Extended family   30
   Family interactions   35, 35–37
   Grandparents roles   49
   Status and hierarchy   34
Feeding   50–51
   Baby food   50–51
   Breast-feeding   50
   Weaning   50
Fengshui   92, 108
Food and diet   51–52, 93–94, 100–101, 107
   Nutrition   94–95

G

Gender differences   60
Gender roles   31, 33, 47–48
Generation gap   48
Gift giving   26–27, 112
Greetings   26

H

Health   90–94
   Causation of illness   92–93
      Supernatural   97, 108
   Healing approaches   93–95, 98
      Acupuncture   95–97, 97
      Folk treatments   93–94
      Herbalism   93, 95, 96, 98
      Therapeutic massage   94
      Traditional treatments   97
   Maintaining health   91–92
   Medicines   93
      Traditional Chinese medicine   95–97
      Vitamins and tonics   95
Health care   103
Heritage language school. *See* Education
Heritage school   46

I

Immigration and Nationality Act   13
Immigration history   12–13, 74
   Communist rule   13
   Economic opportunities   13
   Entry quotas   13
   Political instability   13
   Refugees   13
Intermediary   21
Intervention   108–109
Intra-group diversity   59
Islam. *See* Belief systems

K

Kinships   31–32

L

Language   15–16, 21, 25,
      72, 79, 86, 87, 111
   Cantonese   15–16, 80
   Mandarin   15, 80
   Putonghua   16
   Written language   16
      Pinyin   16
      Traditional script   16
Losing "face"   21, 111

M

Mandarin. *See* Language
Marriage   32, 32–33
   Marital roles and responsibilities   32, 32–33
Mealtimes   52–53
Mental health   91, 92, 99, 104
Music lessons. *See* Education: Extracurricular activities

N

Names   22–23, 68, 85
   English name   24
   Given name   23
      Meanings   23
   Married name   23
   Nicknames   24
   Sequence of names   22
Numbers   26–27

P

Parental pressure. *See* Parenting: Parental
pressure
Parenting   35–37, 54–56
  Baby carrying   49–50
  Feeding   51
  Parent-child interactions   35, 42–
    43, 55, 106
  Parental pressure   43, 64, 74, 75, 77
  Parental roles and responsibilities   42–
    43, 53
  Caregiving   49
Physical contact   26
Pinyin. *See* Language
Polytheism. *See* Belief systems
Population statistics   15
Poverty   76
Pregnancy
  Postpartum care   100, 107
Professional credibility   60–61, 65–
    66, 82, 88, 103, 110
Putonghua. *See* Language

Q

qi   90, 91

R

Relationships outside family   37
Religion. *See* Belief systems

S

School uniforms   68
Sexuality   101
  Homosexuality   101
Siblings   34
Sleeping patterns   53
Smile   *See* Communication style
Special education   106, 110

T

Taoism. *See* Belief systems
Toilet training   53

V

Value Systems   20

Y

yin and yang   90–91, 99, 100, 102